INSIDE STORY

INSIDE STORY

52 Weeks in the Word

TonyaAnn

MEDIA.COM

INSIDE
STORY

Scripture quotations marked (CEV) are from the Contemporary English Version Copyright © 1991, 1992, 1995 by American Bible Society, Used by Permission.

Scripture quotations marked (ESV) are from TheH oly Bible, English Standard Version® (ESV®), copyright © 2001 by Crossway, a publishing ministry of Good News Publishers. Used by permission. All rights reserved.

Scripture is taken from GOD'S WORD®, © 1995 God's Word to the Nations. Used by permission of God's Word Mission Society.

Scripture quotations marked (NIV) are taken from the Holy Bible, New International Version®, NIV®. Copyright © 1973, 1978, 1984, 2011 by Biblica, Inc.™ Used by permission of Zondervan. All rights reserved worldwide. www.zondervan.com The"NIV"and "New International Version" are trademarks registered in the United States Patent and Trademark Office by Biblica, Inc.™

Scripture quotations marked (NLT) are taken from the Holy Bible, New Living Translation, copyright ©1996, 2004, 2007, 2013 by Tyndale House Foundation. Used by permission of Tyndale House Publishers, Inc., Carol Stream, Illinois 60188. All rights reserved.

Scripture quotations marked (TLB) are taken from TheLivingB ible copyright © 1971. Used by permission of Tyndale House Publishers, Inc., Carol Stream, Illinois 60188. All rights reserved.

The vie ws and opinions expressed in this book are those of the author and do not necessarily refle ct offici al policy or position of Illumify Media Global.

Published by
Illumify Media Global
www.IllumifyMedia.com
"We bring your book to life!"

Library of Congress Control Number: 2021915790

Paperback ISBN:978-1-955043-26-7
eBook ISBN: 978-1-955043-27-4

Typeset by Art Innovations (http://artinnovations.in/)
Cover design by Debbie Lewis

Printed in the United States of America

For my sister-cousin in heaven, Lavella: you always knew I could write it, encouraged me in the face of discouragement, and wanted this for me more than I wanted it for myself.

CONTENTS

FOREWORD

It has been my pleasure to know TonyaAnn Pember for more than twenty years in a cherished friendship that blossomed from a church acquaintance to serving together in ministry to a partnership in prayer and a shared love of the Holy Scripture. TonyaAnn brings joy to all facets of her life! She has invested that joy into a beautiful Bible study in her book, *Inside Story: 52 Weeks in The Word.* I have witnessed the fruit of this study in her own life, in the lives of her grown children, and in the lives of her grandchildren. In the weekly devotionals, TonyaAnn guides the reader to a deeper understanding of both sacred and common principles that are easily understood in the Christian faith journey at any level. Drawing on her life experiences, TonyaAnn is able to bring transcendent wisdom to a practical level. The Scripture readings and teachings provide the story of God's love for humanity, from Genesis to Revelation, and the gift of Christ's redemption in each week's entry. The reader will gain knowledge and personal growth as TonyaAnn helps them discover life-changing treasures of truth in Scripture!

— **Rev. Chaplain Beverly Robertson**
Oklahoma City, Oklahoma

INTRODUCTION

"What God has said isn't only alive and active! It is
sharper than any double-edged sword"

(Hebrews 4:12 cev).

I've known this my entire life. I grew up in the church.
My parents were lay people who volunteered for whatever the
church needed. If the doors were open, we were there. I duti-
fully memorized memory verses weekly. As a voracious reader,
I frequently resolved to read the Bible through, but King James
and I were unable to make a connection.

As an adult, I knew I had to read my Bible more. I understood the urgency to know the Word so as not to be misled. I
plodded through Genesis to Revelation, getting lost in the wilderness with the children of Israel somewhere in Deuteronomy.
I marched through the *Chronological Bible*, in several translations, with much the same result. I tried other plans and books
that allowed random Old and New Testament readings with
a Psalm thrown in for good measure. Books that offered daily
devotions, weekly devotions, discussion questions, and journal
questions. I wanted something that would be easier and make

me feel less guilty. I wanted to love God's Word and enjoy reading it. So, I developed and wrote it. You hold it in your hands. My "something different" *Inside Story: 52 Weeks in the Word* invites you to read the entire Bible in one year by genre: Gospels, law, history, wisdom, prophecies, and letters. You choose the Bible translation to read, the day and week to begin, and the method for using the suggested questions. You will spend one week in each genre beginning in *your* new year: January 1 or June 1 or September 1.

Genre reading will help ease confusing sections. Through this progression, you will come closer to understanding the Bible as the ancients wrote it. You will understand the human writers and their texts. Each week begins with a factual introduction to the week's reading called "Learn." The weekly reading, the "Read" portion, will insure you stay on track. Then you will "Consider" my thoughts about the reading and "Respond" to the questions. Your responses may be used for journaling, discussion, and/or self-reflection.

From "In the beginning" to "Come, Lord Jesus," there are many truths and applications possible from this Book of Books. As I researched, studied, read, and wrote, I prayed that the Holy Spirit would reveal himself to each reader individually. As John described regarding all the things Jesus did during His ministry, if we were to try to apply everyone's life to the Scriptures, "I suppose that even the whole world would not have room for the books that would be written" (John 21:25 NIV).

ACKNOWLEDGMENTS

My children, Brittany, Dustin, Nathan, and Lissa: you said, "Do it, Mom," more times than I could count.

My prayer team, Bev, Joleta, Joyce, Loretta, Patty, Tina: you jumped right on board this out-of-control ship and held on for the ride with me.

Mike Klassen and the gang at Illumify Media Global.

The Gospel According To The Tax Collector

LEARN

The first week of reading begins with the story that makes all other stories possible: the Gospels, the stories of Jesus Christ, the one whose life runs through every book of the Bible. It is fitting to begin with Him.

It is believed that Matthew's Gospel was the first written of the four. Matthew, the tax collector, hated among the Jews and used by the Romans. Matthew's Gospel is the most systematic arrangement of Jesus' teaching, expected of a man with mathematical and logical ability. As a disciple, Matthew provides eyewitness accounts of Jesus' time on Earth. Additionally, Matthew wrote from his experience as a Jewish man. He was doubtless schooled in the Old Testament writings. He wrote for his Jewish brothers focusing on the fulfillment of the Old Testament prophecies.

In this week's reading we will read an introduction to the Messiah, as well as the beginning of His ministry. Notice how many times Matthew writes, "You have heard it said . . ." There are more than twenty-five Old Testament references in these nineteen chapters. Matthew was clearly tying the two writings together. Meet the Messiah, Jesus.

READ

Day One	Matthew 1-2
Day Two	Matthew 3-4
Day Three	Matthew 5-7
Day Four	Matthew 8-10
Day Five	Matthew 11-13
Day Six	Matthew 14-16
Day Seven	Matthew 17-19

CONSIDER

The week's passages contain much about our Savior and Lord. We meet Him as a babe in a manger, catch a glimpse of his childhood in Bethlehem, Egypt, and Nazareth. We hear the report of his cousin preparing the way for Him to begin His ministry in fulfillment of Isaiah's prophecies. We read proof of His humanity in the verses regarding His temptation. Midweek we begin to hear His very words.

In a red-letter Bible, there are pages and pages of red. Matthew seems to have quoted Jesus at every turn. He didn't want to share the gospel from his point of view; he wanted Jesus to speak. He wanted the heart of Jesus to be the message of his writing. He instructs the reader how to pray, not to judge, not to worry, how to fast, and did it all while referencing the Old Testament. In these readings, we see Jesus heal the sick and raise the dead. Matthew introduces us to parables. We are reminded that Jesus predicted His own death.

The Gospels easily apply themselves to our culture. The Jews of Jesus' day obeyed laws out of fear of retribution in the synagogue. They were burdened by the rules of sacrifice, sabbath, and outward cleanliness. We, too, are burdened by "law" in the garment of tradition. Some invoke the name of Jesus to push a political agenda or a social one. Jesus is not the face of a political party or an activist group. He had a purpose beyond right and wrong but did not disregard right and wrong. He said so in Matthew 5:17 (NLT): "Don't misunderstand why I have come. I did not come to abolish the law of Moses or the writings of the prophets. No, I came to accomplish their purpose."

Jesus makes it clear that He is not discounting the Old Testament. Donald Stamps *Full Life Study Bible*, now *FireBible*, notes that "Faith in Christ is the point of departure for the fulfilling of the law. Through faith in Christ, God becomes our Father, so our obedience is now out of relationship to him."[1] We obey because we want to please Him, not out of fear of punishment. We have ultimate freedom in Christ; we must use it wisely.

RESPOND

What does Jesus mean when he says he "came to accomplish [the prophets'] purpose"?

Is He referring to a specific law in his reference? Elaborate.

What do you do in your life in Christ that fulfills the law? Give examples of how the law is fulfilled in your life.

Just a Closer Walk with Thee

LEARN

From the beginning of the Gospels to the beginning of the Bible, Genesis. In this the first book of the Bible, we read of creation and the origins of sin, civilization, and humanity. This week we will learn about Abraham and his sons, Ishmael and Isaac. It is widely accepted that Moses is the author of this book and of the next four books of the Law, collectively known as the Pentateuch. This book is the foundation for biblical revelation.

A first reading makes it seem to be almost a book of the history of the world. However, a thorough reading helps it make more sense. From the very beginning God was establishing order in His creation. Rules of nature such as fruit that bears seed and fruit and men that both multiply. The sea had sea creatures and the air had birds. These laws of nature are accepted even among the most skeptical.

Moses may be the author, but Scripture infers that the account of Adam through Joseph was taken from written and oral accounts of others. Eleven times, the text reads, "This is the account of . . ." Moses' Egyptian education and inspiration from God gives him credibility in his writings. As well, Jesus and the apostles verified the accuracy of these writings. Read this week focusing on the natural laws presented.

READ

Day One	Genesis 1-3
Day Two	Genesis 4-7
Day Three	Genesis 8-11
Day Four	Genesis 12-15
Day Five	Genesis 16-19
Day Six	Genesis 20-23
Day Seven	Genesis 24-27

CONSIDER

In the faith hall of fame, Abraham and Sarah are champions. In Hebrews 11:17–19 the author of Hebrews gives a summary of Genesis 22:1–19. He writes about Abraham's willingness to leave home and family and travel in tents with the promised land just over the next hill. Sarah gave birth to a son long after her natural body gave out. Then God asked Abraham to offer his miracle son as a sacrifice. This summary does not do justice to this story. Often we who know this story miss some of the finer points:

"Sometime later"—Isaac wasn't a baby when this happened. He was probably a tweenager. He had watched numerous sacrifices and was schooled in the laws of the same.

Abraham and Isaac traveled *three* days to the place of sacrifice. For three days, Abraham trudged the path with his only son beside him, knowing what he would do when he got there.

Abraham "tied" his son to the altar. Isaac was being taught total submission by a God-fearing father.

The pulpit commentary calls this "heroic faith." That doesn't seem a strong enough word. For both Abraham and Isaac, their faith had taught them not to argue with God, just to obey. Even to the point of death.

For some of you reading this, it is "sometime later" in your life. You have heard this story many times in many presentations. You have known and experienced difficult events that required obedience beyond your desires. You've had to surrender control over your health when the report wasn't good. Over your marriage when your spouse left. Over your finances when the market crashed. Over your children when they turned from their training. And while you understand the significance of three days, it has seemed much longer than that.

Today, in the absence of the need for "heroic faith," think about what happened next in this story, and in that other sto-

ry about a sacrificed son and three days. God spoke. He called
Abraham's name and then provided an alternative sacrifice. Listen, is that your name you hear? The answer is on the way.

RESPOND

Define *submission* for yourself.

Have you ever experienced "heroic faith" or known someone
who has? What did it look like?

Listen for God to call your name. What is He saying to you?

Over and Over and Over Again

LEARN

The entire Old Testament could be considered history, but biblical scholars have called thirteen books, Joshua through Esther, the historical books. Our reading begins with Joshua this week and slips into the beginning of Judges.

Joshua writes his autobiography in this book. The Israelites are camped on the plains of Moab, Moses has died, and God commissions Joshua to take his place. They are preparing to enter Canaan, but they must cross the Jordan River first. The book covers twenty-five to thirty years of history focusing on the fulfillment of God's promise to the Israelites. God appears to Joshua as a man of war. He had never appeared to anyone in that capacity before. The land will be taken by force. The battles are documented in these readings. Once conquered, the inheritance is divided, and refuge cities and Levite cities are assigned. Joshua lives a good, long life, has many years at rest with the nation, and is buried in the "land of his inheritance" (Joshua 24:30 NIV).

In this promised land, the nation is ruled by judges appointed by God. True to their pattern, these Israelites once again oppose God's system. The book of Judges, written by an unknown author, begins with tales of Israel's disobedience. It chronicles their downward spiral into sin and oppression. Read focusing on God's faithfulness to his covenants with Israel.

READ

Day One	Joshua 1–5
Day Two	Joshua 6–10
Day Three	Joshua 11–15
Day Four	Joshua 16–20
Day Five	Joshua 21–24
Day Six	Judges 1–6
Day Seven	Judges 7–11

CONSIDER

The account of the Israelites has startling contrasts to the America of today. Over and over historians note two concerning trends. First, the Israelites did not inquire of the Lord, and second, Israel sinned in the sight of the Lord.

History records that when Israel and its leaders obeyed the Word of God, they were successful in their exploits. However, defeat occurred when they repeatedly refused to ask God for his guidance. As many translations say, they "did not seek the Lord's counsel." Clearly, seeking God's opinion on the battle was paramount.

Following their success in battle, they would be at peace until "the people of Israel did again what was evil." Back to war, over and over again. It's easy to judge these people. They had Moses' testimony, they had Joshua's leadership, they had tasted victory. There was no doubt they knew how to live in prosperity, but "they did again what was evil."

During political unrest, all sides often claim to be "Christian." Some politicians claim to be "born again." In these times, the church can become divided due to the arrogance of all parties. We say with Joshua, "Are you one of us or one of our enemies?" (Joshua 5:13 GW). Hear the answer and imagine God speaking it today, "Neither one! I am here as the commander of the LORD's army" (Joshua 5:14 GW).

God is neither for the donkey nor for the elephant. He is here for Himself. *The Pulpit Commentary* suggests that when God arrives for "neither," "it is because the battle is so intense, only God Himself could save now."[2] The battle for Jericho was intense as is the battle for America. It's time we inquired of the Lord.

RESPOND

What do you see as the most intense battle in our country today?

What might happen if you gathered a few friends to "inquire of the Lord"?

What are some ways you could help your government and/ or church leadership "inquire of the Lord"?

Promises and Proclamations

LEARN

This week's readings will center on the center of the Bible: the Psalms. The first forty-one Psalms conclude by giving praise to Yahweh, the Lord. Most of the first twenty Psalms were written by King David. They are the writings of an author's deep emotions and inner thoughts and conflicts. They are generally short, easy-to-read passages. That can make the reader complacent and less likely to see the deeper meanings. The entire book of Psalms is a book of worship. The God of the law and of all history and prophecies is deserving of worship.

Later in the week we will mix in a little history and begin reading the book of Deuteronomy. The first twenty Psalms and Deuteronomy are not related in time but related in life. Deuteronomy was written for the new generation of Israelites preparing to enter Canaan. Moses takes this opportunity to remind them of their history and obligations. He encourages them to fear the

Lord, walk in His ways, and love and honor their God. Many of
the Psalms express those feelings. Experience these Psalms while
considering the laws of God.

READ

Day One	Psalm 1-6
Day Two	Psalm 7-12
Day Three	Psalm 13-17
Day Four	Psalm 18-20
Day Five	Deuteronomy 1-2
Day Six	Deuteronomy 3-4
Day Seven	Deuteronomy 5-6

CONSIDER

The first twenty chapters of prayer and praise in the Psalms
mirror the Christian's everyday life. The author cries out in anguish and then shouts out in faith. The most reassuring of these
words promise His faithfulness to all generations. It's a promise
written about in Deuteronomy in the form of an if-then promise. For example, if you do this, I, God, will do that. As an Israelite family, David's parents would have hearkened back to the
words of Moses in Deuteronomy 4:9 (NIV): "Only be careful,
and watch yourselves closely so that you do not forget the things
your eyes have seen or let them fade from your heart as long

as you live. Teach them to your children and to their children after them." David would have known the Israeli history and was likely schooled in the books of the Law. Of course, his songs would have included thanksgiving for God's mercy and faithfulness. It was natural to admonish himself (and us) to serve and honor the Lord. To trust in the Lord.

We can relate to David's cries in Psalm 12:1 (NIV): "Help, O LORD, for the godly are fast disappearing. The faithful have vanished from the earth!" But the psalmist's words of heartache, sorrow, and fear are always bookended with faith: "The LORD watches over the way of the righteous" (Psalm 1:6 NIV); "Blessed are all who take refuge in Him" (Psalm 2:12 NIV); "From the Lord comes deliverance" (Psalm 3:8 NIV); "You will fill me with joy in your presence" (Psalm 16:11 NIV). We can rest in the promises from Deuteronomy and the proclamations from Psalms.

RESPOND

How could you teach your children, whatever age (even adult), a truth of God this week?

Choose three proclamations from the Psalms reading to apply to your life today.

Do you feel that the "godly are fast disappearing" from our culture? Why or why not?

Why Me, Lord?

LEARN

The book of Job is classified as wisdom and poetry. It is considered wisdom because it deals with an important question, perhaps the most profound question of the Bible: why do the righteous suffer? The writer of the book is a mystery and its date uncertain. Scholars believe Job wrote this autobiography about the same time as Abraham was living in Ur. Whoever and whenever, the author was under divine inspiration and had detailed information about the events detailed in the book. The book of Job is possibly the most famous book of the Bible. This righteous man, Job, could have sung the common lament, "Why, me, Lord?" However, God championed him as an example on the earth. His three friends, Eliphaz, Bildad, and Zophar, had differing opinions on why Job was having such a hard life, but all agreed he must be a hypocrite. Focus on Job's friends as you read this week.

READ

CONSIDER

Job was "blameless and upright; he feared God and shunned evil" (Job 1:1 NIV). Satan obviously tried to infiltrate his life because in Job 1:9 he pointed out to God the hedge around Job and his household. Much has been written about Job, his trials, the conversations that ensued between him, God, and his friends. These friends are not written about with much respect. In fact, they are usually the example of cruelty and legalism. Perhaps the book of Job is a commentary on friendship as well as suffering. Let's take a closer look at those friends.

In this week's reading, we meet three of Job's friends. When they "heard about all the troubles that had come upon him," they came to see him (Job 2:11 NIV). After the death of a loved one or some other crisis, many friends and acquaintances reach out. They fill the house, but in a few days it goes quiet. Friends don't know what to say and don't want to add to the sorrow. So they offer the afflicted "space." Job comes down with some unknown disease with sores all over his body, looking hideous. His own wife ridicules him. Doubtless, other acquaintances have deserted him. He is the talk of the town, he looks so grotesque. But these three, they come.

They weep with him and sit with him for seven days. They are friends who simply sit with Job. At first they don't try to fix anything, no words of comfort; they are just present. Sometimes we need someone to sit with us, cry with us, and acknowledge our feelings whether they are "right" or not. These guys are real friends. Until, after a week, Job speaks, and his words are not pleasant, hopeful words. The previously sympathetic friends soon turn to accusations, faulty theology, and disputes about Job's character.

Eliphaz the Temanite speaks first. Teman was a region known for its wisdom. These people believed that God was impartial and dispensed judgment based on the recipient's behavior. Eliphaz was a religious extremist. He relied on human experience for his belief. In his first speech to Job, he courteously but firmly informs Job that this calamity is a result of his sin. Judge and jury.

Bildad speaks next, imploring Job to repent of his sin. He implies that prosperity is a direct link to one's righteousness. Job would not be in so much agony if he didn't have hidden sin in his life. Bildad was a descendant of Abraham and rooted his beliefs in human tradition and the history of his lineage.

Along comes Zophar. The most adamant of the three. Zophar is a legalist, believing human merit is the answer to suffering. Suffering is judgment, and clearly Job is under judgment. He rubs salt in the wound by proclaiming that Job deserves far more punishment.

Unfortunately, these three aren't through talking, but we'll come back to them in a few weeks.

RESPOND

What would Satan say about you to God?

Which of Job's friends' beliefs align with yours?

Think of a time when you have suffered. Which one of these friend personalities came? How did that make you feel?

The Hezekiah Process

LEARN

Week six leads us into the minefield of prophecy, which is defined by Dictionary.com as "a divinely inspired prediction, instruction, or exhortation" delivered by a prophet. Isaiah was a prophet during the reign of four Judean kings from 700 to 680 BC. His writings encompass prediction, instruction, and exhortation. Isaiah wrote for three different purposes. He first addressed the sin of his own nation. In his first chapters, he prophesied hope to the Jewish exiles and hope to the world through the Messiah.

In the very first verse of Isaiah 1 (NIV), he announces "the vision concerning Judah and Jerusalem." This week's readings will encompass prophecies of judgment and rebuke both for the Israelites and for us. Isaiah will hint of the Messiah and his coming kingdom. Sadly, most of our reading will not be hopeful, as Isaiah foretells judgment against the nations by name. Buckle up!

READ

Day One	Isaiah 1–6
Day Two	Isaiah 7–11
Day Three	Isaiah 12–17
Day Four	Isaiah 18–22
Day Five	Isaiah 23–28
Day Six	Isaiah 29–33
Day Seven	Isaiah 34–39

CONSIDER

Isaiah begins with bad news in the form of a message from the Lord: "They have rebelled against me" (Isaiah 1:2 NIV). These chapters do not seem like "history"; they seem like current events.

America, like Isaiah's Israel, is a rebellious nation. As they did, we have rebelled against God. We have blatantly ignored His commands, elevated men and money and corporations above Him. We revere athletes and actors more than we revere God. Our devotion to our jobs, sports teams, and political parties outweighs our devotion to God. As George Santayana said, "Those who cannot remember the past are condemned to repeat it."[3] Is it possible America is repeating the history of the Israelites? Isaiah's words should convict us.

At the end of this week's scriptures, we read the story of Hezekiah. *The Full Life Study Bible* calls chapters 36–39 a "historical interlude concerning Hezekiah."[4] A little break from the doom and gloom, Hezekiah starts out strong. He stood up to the lies and insults of the king of Assyria. When he faced trouble, he "tore his clothes and put on sackcloth and went into the temple of the Lord" (Isaiah 37:1 NIV). In the face of continued persecution, he prayed. The time came when a wicked king sent Hezekiah a rather intimidating letter. The wicked king outlined his victories against other nations. He goes as far as to warn Hezekiah, "Do not let the god you depend on deceive you" (Isaiah 37:10 NIV). Hezekiah responds by going to the temple of the Lord. He responds, as we should to the rebellion around us, with a three-point plan.

First he acknowledges who God is. He calls Him the "LORD Almighty, the God of Israel" (Isaiah 37:16 NIV). Then he asks that God see and hear. Hezekiah takes the letter and spreads it out before the Lord. He points out the parts of the letter that are true with a sidebar about that truth. He ends with the faith statement he began with. Hezekiah acknowledges who God is.

RESPOND

Apply Hezekiah's process to an event of your life. In prayer, do the following:

State the facts of what is being said or done.

Are any of the accusations being made factual?

Proclaim to the Lord, as Hezekiah did, "You alone are God" (Isaiah 37:16 NIV).

You've Got Mail

LEARN

The genre of epistles, or letters, is among the most familiar of all scriptures, the easiest to understand, and the most enjoyable to read despite its sometimes harsh instruction. The author of this week's letters is Paul, whom we learn about in the book of Acts.

The nine books authored by Paul were easily recognized as letters. They were structured to make any English teacher proud—beginning with a salutation, then using the body of the letter for thanksgiving, an explanation of the theme needed by each church, and an appeal for change. Each letter concluded with a heartfelt good-bye. Most were hand-signed by Paul to testify to their authenticity. Paul's nine letters encouraged the church of the New Testament (and the church of today) to be victorious, but each letter addressed a specific victory.

We begin our reading of Paul's letters with the longest, most influential, and likely most theological letter: the one he wrote to his countrymen, the Romans. It was written in 57 AD with the purpose of revealing God's righteousness. Paul wanted the Roman church to be victorious over ignorance. He planned to visit them in person and his letter was to prepare them for that visit. Paul uses the Old Testament extensively to prove his presentation of the gospel. Let's read the letter in its entirety this week.

READ

Day One	Romans 1-2
Day Two	Romans 3-5
Day Three	Romans 6-8
Day Four	Romans 9-10
Day Five	Romans 11-12
Day Six	Romans 13-14
Day Seven	Romans 15-16

CONSIDER

Paul's purpose in this letter to the Roman church is to reveal God's righteousness. He accomplishes that in two quite different ways. Paul speaks to the Jews in his audience with Old Testament prophecies and references. He writes to them about Jesus in language and a tradition they can understand. He is equally as discerning in explaining Christ to the Gentiles. He presents the message to them accounting for their cultural traditions and understanding. From the very beginning, God knew that everyone he had formed would need to hear His message in his or her own language. Paul demonstrates this in the book of Romans.

Those among us with little if any knowledge of the church, the Word, or traditions of American Christianity do not speak church vernacular. Presenting the truth of Jesus requires the message in one's own language. Not language like English, French, or Spanish necessarily, but in a language that appeals to the reader's personality, background, and values. Paul speaks with a vocabulary specific to each person. He sends specific messengers to a specific audience. For example, when we say, "You're speaking my language," your life experience is the story I need to hear. You are the one to bring the message of Christ to a specific audience.

RESPOND

What experiences, traditions, or values are unique to your family?

What "language" led you to salvation?

How could you share your favorite scripture in someone else's "language"?

I Will Change Your Name

LEARN

This week we return to the Gospels, specifically the final nine chapters of Matthew and the first eight of Mark.

When last we left Matthew, Jesus was preparing to spend his final week on Earth and had begun his journey to Jerusalem. In true Matthew fashion, he recounts this harrowing week with little emotion and just the facts. His report is short on detail, but he manages to describe Peter's denial and Judas's suicide. It's a story mentioned in all four gospels with the same facts but different approaches.

John Mark was born and raised in Jerusalem in a wealthy Jewish family. His Gospel was written after Jesus' resurrection and possibly after his infamous abandonment of Barnabus and Paul (that story is coming). Mark was associated with the New Testament apostles but especially close to Simon Peter. Scholars believe his accounts are based on Simon's reports. It is the shortest of the Gospels and believed to be the first written. Mark was more interested in what Jesus did than what he said. His Gospel emphasizes the opposition of the Pharisees and gives details that only Peter could have known. He saw Jesus as a servant willing to sacrifice even His own life.

In this week's reading, Mark will give us insight into Jesus' preparation for His mission as that servant. He begins in Capernaum. Let's travel a few miles with Jesus.

READ

Day One	Matthew 20–22
Day Two	Matthew 23–25
Day Three	Matthew 26–28
Day Four	Mark 1–2
Day Five	Mark 3–4
Day Six	Mark 5–6
Day Seven	Mark 7–8

CONSIDER

Mark has a story to tell, and he gets right to it. His writings spend no time at all on Jesus' birth, lineage, or early days. He presents Jesus as a servant, and as Jabe Nicholson says, "No one concerns himself with the heritage of a servant."[5] Mark starts with the ministry of John the Baptist and the temptation of Jesus. He recounts many miracles and retells many parables. Mark emphasizes that Jesus is concerned with Satan and his demonic powers. Jesus observed them firsthand, as we read about in Mark 1. Mark records Jesus' authority over these demons as well.

In chapter 8, Jesus asks his disciples, "Who do people say I am?" (Mark 8:27 NIV). Matthew, Mark, and Luke record their answers identically. When Jesus asks, "Who do you say I am?" in verse 29, the same three record that Simon Peter answered, "You are the Messiah " (Mark 8:29 NIV). All three record that He warned them not to tell anyone. Only Matthew writes what Jesus said to Simon, changing his name to Peter.

In Mark's version, he attributes the proclamation "You are the Christ" to Peter. Obviously, Mark knew that Simon was now Peter. It's possible that Mark only knew him as Peter. Jesus changed his name in response to his confession.

What's in a name? History records that Simon before Jesus was somewhat of a scoundrel. Not always honest, impulsive, and stubborn. This man who had been with Jesus was no longer that person. This man was different because of Christ, a new creation, a rock, Peter.

What's in a name? For some of you, you've been given a name that has destroyed your heart. "Unworthy, unloved, unwanted, unable." These are names that Jesus also changes. When we confess that He is Christ, Savior, Redeemer, and Friend, He changes our names. He calls us Loved, Blessed, and Chosen. That's what's in the name given to God's children.

RESPOND

What does your name mean? Why were you given it?

How would others describe your life?

Who is this Jesus to you?

In the Beginning,
Part Two

LEARN

It's back to the beginning this week, to Genesis, to complete the story of the third patriarch. A patriarch is regarded as the founder or father to a class of people. Obviously, the Jews consider Abraham, Isaac, and Jacob as their patriarchs. In these twenty-two chapters of Genesis, we read the story of Jacob. Previously, we read that Jacob has fled to Laban to escape the wrath of his brother, Esau, and to find a wife among his own people. The trip is not easy, but it is filled with God's direction. The deceiver is deceived and ends up with an unwanted wife. Two wives and two mistresses later, he has twelve sons. These become the twelve tribes of Israel. Let's read a little bit about all the boys but one in particular who stands out. It's a familiar story to the Christian. Search for something new this week.

READ

Day One	Genesis 28-31
Day Two	Genesis 32-35
Day Three	Genesis 36-39
Day Four	Genesis 40-41
Day Five	Genesis 42-43
Day Six	Genesis 44-47
Day Seven	Genesis 48-50

CONSIDER

These chapters are considered law, but they are rich in history and prophecy. This is a second "in the beginning," as the readings chronicle the beginning of the chosen people of God. These readings form a foundation for the entire Old Testament and its relevance to the New. Down through the ages, we hear of the conflict between Edom and Judah. In the years to come, the Israelites will be slaves in Egypt. The twelve tribes of Israel will acquire promised land according to their tribe. Most of their names will be overshadowed by their more famous brother, Joseph.

In these chapters, we understand how the twelve tribes of Israel came to be, led by the twelve sons of Jacob. Moses gives us detail after detail regarding Jacob's marriages and the births of his sons. Jacob must take Leah to get Rachel. The two of them add their maids into the mix out of jealousy. Jacob loved Rachel but was not fond of Leah. Genesis tells us that God gave Leah children but Rachel was barren. In desperation Rachel demanded Jacob sleep with her servant Bilhah. After Bilhah bore two sons, Leah was too old to bear more children, so she gave her servant Zilpah to Jacob. Twelve boys are born into the family with four different mothers. Leah is a mocker, Rachel is a thief, Jacob a deceiver, and those boys, they all had their faults. This family history is a roller coaster of trouble, good times, famine, feast, lies, and deceit. The story would be rated PG-13 at best.

In fact, the story sounds like life in the twenty-first century. Argumentative spouses, bickering kids, cheating employers, hard work for little pay, false accusations, broken promises. Jacob's story is not so different from our own. Yet it is part of a bigger plan. Jacob's infidelities bore the people of God. The brothers' jealousy sent Joseph to Egypt. While there, Joseph developed an uncanny knack for interpreting dreams that put him into a leadership position. Ironically, Pharoah's dream gave Joseph the ability to live his dream. It led to reuniting with his brothers and bringing them to live in Egypt. Here, they, too, were honored by Pharoah and given the land of Goshen. No wonder Joseph could proclaim, "You intended to harm me, but God intended it for good to accomplish what is now being done, the saving of many lives" (Genesis 50:20 NIV).

Two thousand years later, a descendant of Judah, an Israelite Jew, would also save many lives. This is only the beginning of the story.

RESPOND

Which of the three patriarchs can you relate to? Why?

What is happening right now in your life that seems "harmful"?

Has there been a time in your experience where something bad turned out good? Explain.

Paradox

LEARN

We continue to probe the history of the Jewish people this week beginning with the difficulties of their enemies living in the promised land. We will read a familiar story of Philistine oppression and view the idolatry, immorality, and strife among the tribes of Israel. These readings are a clear picture into the consequences that occur when we forget the Lord and live for our own selfish desires. Consider the sins of Israel and how they equate with the sins of America.

On a happier note, we will read the story of Ruth. Another familiar story that deserves a deeper look. Women are the main characters in only two books of the Bible, Esther being the other. Ruth's story is a description of an Israelite family living during the time of the Judges. The Talmud credits Samuel with writing this book, but Scripture does not identify him. The theme of this story is Redemption. Ruth is identified with our great Redeemer because of her offspring.

READ

Day One	Judges 12–13
Day Two	Judges 14–15
Day Three	Judges 16–17
Day Four	Judges 18–19
Day Five	Judges 20–21
Day Six	Ruth 1–2
Day Seven	Ruth 3–4

CONSIDER

This week's reading is a paradox as we compare these last chapters of Judges and the book of Ruth. The paradox is in the difference between the stories' outcomes. The last ten chapters of Judges continue the saga of war, sin, and depravity among the Israelites. Much of this reading is the story of Samson. Born into the clan of Dan during the Philistine oppression, Samson was set apart by his parents for God from birth. Unfortunately, it's the story of how the good can go bad. Although Samson knew his birthright, he treated it with little respect. He disregarded his parents' counsel and thought highly of himself. He repeatedly gave in to his own desires especially where women were involved. In Judges 16:20 (NIV), Scripture tells us "that the LORD had left him." He was so sure of himself, he didn't even notice until the Philistines bound him. Even when God showed His might through Samson's death in the temple of Dagon, the people of Israel "did as they saw fit" (Judges 17:6 NIV). The entire nation decided their own version of right and wrong. This inevitably leads to evil in God's eyes.

Contrast this story with the story of Ruth. Ruth was a woman not of Israelite descent, no knowledge of the Israelite law and history. Yet she chose to align herself with these foreigners, unlike her sister-in-law, Orpha. Out of respect, she chose to hear the wisdom of her mother-in-law and follow her directions. Her faithfulness created a future for both women. In the last chapter of Ruth, the author finds it necessary to include the lineage of Ruth's husband, Boaz. Note the reference to "Jesse, the father of David," Ruth's great grandson (Ruth 4:17 NIV). It's easy to see the significance of this information as David becomes Israel's greatest king. Look down through the ages and notice another "more excellent" King in this lineage.

We live in a world that has blurred the lines between right and wrong. However, the Word of God has not blurred those lines; we are still responsible to His definition. Samson chose to walk as close as possible to the edge of "wrong." Ruth chose to accept another culture's values and walk to the "right." There are only two choices.

RESPOND

How do you relate to Samson's story regarding your own childhood and/or young adulthood?

Think of or list five events that illustrate our nation doing "as we see fit."

What is the purpose of Ruth's story in holy Scripture?

Remind Me

LEARN

This week we continue in Psalms and Deuteronomy. The passages in Deuteronomy describe the people of Israel as they approach Canaan. Throughout the book, Moses reviews and renews God's commands for these young Israelites. Our reading will include the Commandments, the Shema, and the obligations of the Covenant made with God. The ancient words of Moses were inscribed upon the hearts of young Jewish boys. Jesus was no different. When He was tempted by Satan in the wilderness, he quoted Deuteronomy 6:13, 6:16, and 8:3.

Although Psalms 21–41 are not the Psalms of this time period, the Israelites doubtless would have proclaimed joy in this journey, praise for the land before them and trust in the God who had brought them so far. Seven times in these Psalms, the author says, "Teach me." The book of Deuteronomy is the answer to this request.

READ

Day One	Deuteronomy 7-9
Day Two	Deuteronomy 10-11
Day Three	Psalms 21-24
Day Four	Psalms 25-28
Day Five	Psalms 29-32
Day Six	Psalms 33-37
Day Seven	Psalms 38-41

CONSIDER

It's a new experience reading the rules of Deuteronomy and the Psalms of man and creation in the same week. Moses commands the Israelites to hear and obey the commandments, impress them on their hearts, and teach them to their children.

Like Moses, the psalmist in these readings reminds himself of where he has been, of the victories and losses of serving God. And similarly he asks God, "Teach me." Thousands of years later the disciples will ask of Jesus, "Teach us." Biblical characters never tire of being taught by God. It speaks to the vastness and greatness of the God of the universe. These words of His are ancient, and yet the word *ancient* rolls off the tongue with nostalgia. *Ancient*, according to Dictionary.com, means "of or in a long time past; dating from a remote period, of great age." Ancient, by its very definition, speaks of age but also everlasting worth. Everlasting worth. That illustrates what we have read this week. Ancient words applied to our lives change us. They do not change our circumstances, they change us. Ancient words dive deep within us and reverberate in our hearts.

RESPOND

Read Deuteronomy 10:12 again. What does God require of you?

Who "taught" you the ancient words of God? Have you thanked them?

What does it mean to "impress" something upon your heart? What is impressed upon your heart?

With Friends Like These

LEARN

We return to Job again and read the next two cycles of conversation. The first round concentrated on Job in Satan's hands. This second round will discuss a man in men's hands and finally will address a man in God's hands.

Remember the character of each of Job's three friends as you read. Eliphaz is coming down hard, almost cruelly, on Job. He is determined to make Job see the error of his ways. Bildad is concentrating on the failures in Job's history, reminding him of all the things he did wrong in the past. Zophar remains the doomsday predictor of the group. Job continues to maintain his innocence, which only serves to anger his friends even more. As you read this week, imagine each character speaking, think of his heritage and beliefs.

READ

Day One	Job 15–16
Day Two	Job 17–18
Day Three	Job 19–20
Day Four	Job 21–22
Day Five	Job 23–24
Day Six	Job 25–26
Day Seven	Job 27–28

CONSIDER

Job is the epitome of "with friends like these, who needs enemies?" In these chapters, Eliphaz, Zophar, and Bildad continue to build their arguments, but they become more persistent and a lot less kind. They are not completely wrong. In fact, they are just enough right to give themselves some credibility. Eliphaz declares in Job 15:6, "Your own mouth condemns you." Matthew 12:37 (NLT) records Jesus saying much the same: "The words you say will either acquit you or condemn you." Bildad suggests Job's wickedness will cause "his roots [to] dry up below and his branches [to] wither above" (Job 18:16 NIV). Isaiah 5:24 echoes the same punishment for those who reject the law of the Lord. Zophar, in his last claim, points out, as does the psalmist, that the time of the wicked is brief. Much of Job's friends' advice was true, but their doctrine was wrong. Their hearts were also contaminated, and God looks at the heart.

Righteousness does not mean prosperity. Suffering does not imply sinfulness. Job endured the most crushing peer pressure imaginable. His "friends" insisted he repent of sins he had not committed. They condemned him for actions he had not taken and compared his circumstances to historical judgments that were not applicable. Job maintained his faith in God, proclaiming, "I know that my redeemer lives, and that in the end he will stand on the earth" (Job 19:25 NIV).

Amid great suffering and hopelessness, God gave Job discernment. The wisdom to know truth from lies. Job recognized that his friends' opinions were not factual because of what he *knew* about his God.

We live in a world that is ripe with half-truths, innuendos, and untruths. It is crucial that we study, read, and absorb God's Word so that we can recognize truth, the whole truth, and nothing but the truth. While we love and pray for those who do not walk in truth, we must be careful to close our ears to their misrepresentations of truth.

God has not yet spoken into Job's situation. Stick around for a few more weeks.

RESPOND

Given your history, traditions, and beliefs, whom do you identify with most: Eliphaz, Bildad, or Zophar?

Whom do you turn to in a crisis? What makes them your go-to person?

What one thing could you change in your past handling of a friend's crisis?

Some through Great Sorrow

LEARN

Isaiah's final prophecies are about hope, salvation, and restoration. He promises a bright and happy future for the children of Israel. We will enjoy the completion of his book this week. Chapters 50–65 contain many prophecies fulfilled in Jesus Christ. How many can you find during your reading? Hint: there are sixteen.

Thankfully, Isaiah ends on such a hopeful word because Jeremiah sweeps right in at the end of the week. Jeremiah, the "weeping prophet." The voice of doom and gloom. Writing in 585–580 BC, Jeremiah was tasked by God to speak this ruthless message to the people of Judah. He was bold and courageous as he proclaimed the words God gave him. Even so, he was a man of tender spirit and broken heart. It has been said of Jeremiah and his message, "A more crushing burden was never laid upon mortal man."[6] In chapter 1, we read why he took on this burden.

READ

Day One	Isaiah 40-44
Day Two	Isaiah 45-50
Day Three	Isaiah 51-55
Day Four	Isaiah 56-61
Day Five	Isaiah 62-66
Day Six	Jeremiah 1-6
Day Seven	Jeremiah 7-14

CONSIDER

The last twenty-seven chapters of Isaiah provide words of hope for the children of God. That hope radiates from the prophecies concerning the Messiah. Half of the sixteen prophecies occur in chapter 53. Isaiah wrote these words between 700 and 680 BC, and centuries later they were fulfilled in Jesus.

This Jesus was not the good-looking guy portrayed in movies and TV shows. Isaiah predicted he had nothing that would attract men to Him. He wouldn't be accepted by His own people, and they would reject his claims. This would cause Him great suffering but still, He would become the substitute for their/our sentence of death. Isaiah and his people held on to this hope, until the end of their lives.

Isaiah did not live to see this Savior walk upon the earth. He did not live to know his prophecies were fulfilled. He was obedient and trusted in what did not come to pass in his lifetime.

Doubtless you have loved ones who waited for the second coming of this Savior and did not live to see it. Certainly, you have wondered if He will come in your lifetime. Mimic Isaiah's example and walk in obedience, waiting with hope and trust.

RESPOND

How many of the prophecies did you find? Did any of them surprise you?

Has anyone prophesied over you? How did you feel about it? Did it happen, or are you still waiting, perhaps not expecting it to happen?

Do you expect to see Jesus come again? Why or why not?

Tolerance Is Not Righteousness

LEARN

The genre reading plan gives us a chance to toggle between bad news, worse news, hopeful news, and good news. This week we travel to Corinth between 55 and 56 AD and celebrate the Christians there through Paul's eyes. Paul founded the church at Corinth during his second missionary journey. Most of its membership were ex-pagan Gentiles. As a result, they still walked in their worldly desires. Their spiritual immaturity blinded them to the seriousness of their behavior. Paul (and God) desired this church to be victorious over sin. Painful as it was, Paul was obligated to address their questionable behavior. They also had questions about marriage, public worship, the resurrection, tithing, and the use of freedom within the confines of holiness.

This book is especially instructional about the gifts of the Holy Spirit. Paul provides guidelines for the part these gifts play in our church. Further, he addresses how they benefit both the individual and the body of Christ. This letter is addressed to "you who have been called by God to be his own holy people" (1 Corinthians 1:2 NLT). That would be us.

READ

Day One	1 Corinthians 1-3
Day Two	1 Corinthians 4-6
Day Three	1 Corinthians 7-8
Day Four	1 Corinthians 9-10
Day Five	1 Corinthians 11-12
Day Six	1 Corinthians 13-14
Day Seven	1 Corinthians 15-16

CONSIDER

Paul's heart must have been breaking as he penned this letter to a church he had founded and loved. He reminds them right away of their call to holiness and commends them on their spiritual gifts. Then he addresses the divisions among the congregants.

The Corinthian church had lost its focus. There were arguments among them involving which apostle they should follow. They were tolerating evil within the church. There was a rash of jealousy and quarrels. They were in critical danger of conforming to the world, and they were unconcerned about that possibility.

Corinth is a long way from America, but the similarities are chilling. The *Full Life Study Bible* calls the believers at Corinth "worldly Christians."[7] These Christians had not submitted to sin and rebellion. They were not immoral or unrighteous. There were some arguments among them. Most troubling, they were tolerating sin in the name of love. They didn't want to offend by calling out sin among their brethren. They had not conformed to the world, but they were walking a fine line. Paul was filled with grief because of this, and in 1 Corinthians 5:2 he suggests that the church should be also. The lifestyle of Corinth is not so far from America. In the name of tolerance, in fear of "hate speech," we hesitate to speak out against immorality. We ignore racism in the name of "minding our own business." Too many of our leaders are afraid to speak truth for fear of income loss. The evil around us should fill us with grief. And send us to our knees in repentance and petition. Jesus calls these people "lukewarm," and that will not end well.

RESPOND

What divisions can you identify among the church today?

What are some social or cultural ideologies you believe the church is tolerating?

What are your personal beliefs about the list from question two?

It Is Finished

LEARN

As we reopen the book of Mark, we will complete our reading with his account of the sacrifice of Jesus. While he continues to report on Jesus' travels through Galilee, the majority of these scriptures will deal with the final week of Christ's life on Earth. In his conversational style, Mark tells the story with little emotion, just the facts. It is believed that because of Mark's family ties, he was quite possibly in the Sanhedrin for the "trial" and reports as an eyewitness. Mark is the only Gospel writer to write that after Jesus was taken up into Heaven, "he sat at the right hand of God" (Mark 16:19 NIV). Jesus was finished, completed, done. As we will be with the book of Mark midweek.

Completing Mark, we will begin reading the book of Luke. Luke, like Mark, was not a disciple but well acquainted with the apostles. Luke was a Gentile physician, well-educated, an observant historian and prolific writer. His status as a Gentile convert gave him influence with the non-Jewish believers, thus he wrote to provide them with a Gentile record of Jesus Christ. Luke assured his Gentile readers that he had investigated every claim about Jesus. He writes in Luke 1:3 (NLT), "Having carefully investigated everything from the beginning, I also have decided to write an accurate account for you." He begins, at the beginning, with the birth of John the Baptist, then Jesus. This week's rendition will give us an end and a beginning.

READ

Day One	Mark 9-10
Day Two	Mark 11-12
Day Three	Mark 13-14
Day Four	Mark 15-16
Day Five	Luke 1-3
Day Six	Luke 4-6
Day Seven	Luke 7-8

CONSIDER

In Mark 16:19 (ESV), Mark records, "So then the Lord Jesus, after he had spoken to them, was taken up into heaven and he sat at the right hand of God." Not exactly a popular text for sermons. Actually, it happened right after the biggest event in Christian history, the resurrection. The ascension of Jesus into heaven may have seemed anticlimactic at the time. Matthew didn't mention it; Luke mentions it briefly and then references it again in Acts. John alludes to it using Jesus' own words. Mark is the only writer who leaves this sentence. He seems to be writing of something he saw but which did not surprise him. Mark makes two points that merit attention:

"He sat down." Jesus' work was done. He had come in a manager, grew up on the run, learned woodworking at the feet of his earthly father, studied, and ministered. He walked the earth 24/7 for 365 days, ministering, for three years. He endured two trials, nine hours of humiliation, being mocked and tortured until finally being crucified on a common cross. There was still no rest. He descended into Satan's den to defeat him and make sure he knew it. He came out of the tomb victorious and continued to minister for forty more days. He was deserving of the sit-down. He had done what he needed to do to give us salvation.

"At the right hand of God." When a person with high rank (God) sits someone (Jesus) at his right hand, he is saying that this person has equal position, honor, power, and authority with himself. This is documented many times in later scriptures written by Paul, Matthew, John, and Luke. That Jesus is sitting at the right hand of God should be as amazing as any of the things Jesus did for us. The scholar and minister Alexander Maclaren says that this fact alone "should fill the present for us all, even as the Cross should fill the past, and the coming for Judgement should fill the future."[8]

RESPOND

What does the ascension of Christ mean to you?

How does the cross relate to your past?

How do you feel about the coming judgment? Is there something you need to change?

Let My People Go

LEARN

Returning this week to the Law, we launch into the book of Exodus. Moses penned this book to be a historical record of the deliverance of Israel by God. These chapters chronicle the oppression of the Israelites in Egypt as well as announce the birth and life of their liberator. Moses leads us through the wilderness with these wanderers.

The book of Exodus is the foundational book for the nation of Israel. Chapters 1–18 deal with their national foundation. Chapters 19–24 deal with their legislative foundation. In *Explore the Book*, J. Sidlow Baxter makes this week's readings seem exciting: "Is there in all history a more amazing spectacle than the Exodus, a more august and solemn revelation than God at Sinai, a more significant piece of architecture than the Israelite Tabernacle, a greater human figure than the man, Moses?"[9] Judge for yourself.

READ

Day One	Exodus 1-4
Day Two	Exodus 5-8
Day Three	Exodus 9-12
Day Four	Exodus 13-15
Day Five	Exodus 16-18
Day Six	Exodus 19-21
Day Seven	Exodus 22-24

CONSIDER

The book of Exodus is considered God's Law as part of the Pentateuch, but it is also very much a history of the people of Israel. The people of God had settled in a part of Egypt called Goshen. This is recorded in Genesis 46 when Jacob and his boys joined Joseph in Egypt. It was here the Israelites made their home even after they became slaves.

They had been slaves to the Egyptians for four hundred years. Generations had come and gone, and their lives got worse. Adding insult to injury, the older ones continued to pass on the story of coming deliverance. Coupled with their alleged deliverer, an Israelite-raised Egyptian named Moses, returning to Egypt and making things worse by offending the Pharoah, these people had reason to be discouraged.

Scholars differ on whether the Israelites were protected from the plagues that beset the Egyptians. Exodus 8:22 states, " But on that day I will deal differently with the land of Goshen, where my people live; no swarms of flies will be there." This is the first time there is any mention that the Israelites were spared these annoyances. It's possible their "deliverance" included being subjected to the first three plagues. It begins when all the water in Egypt turns to blood: "Blood was everywhere in Egypt" (Exodus 7:21 NIV) . Within a week, "frogs came up and covered the land" (Exodus 8:6 NIV). After they cleaned up all the dead frogs and piled them in stinking heaps, "All the dust throughout the land of Egypt became gnats" (Exodus 8:17 NIV).

The word *exodus* means "to exit." Even after their "deliverer," Moses, had come, there were many days before the exit. And then it came in the middle of the night, and they had to leave quickly. Moving 2.4 million people from one place to another was a massive undertaking. They succeed, however, and days later find themselves on the bank of the rushing Red Sea, hemmed in by mountains on the right and left and the Egyptian army to their back. Yes, on top of all they had already endured, now they are in a corner. They don't yet know they will spend the next forty years wandering around the desert. Undoubtedly, the Israelites considered life in Egypt, bad as it was, better than this. They wanted to go back; this would not be the last time these people would feel this way.

RESPOND

What "plague" plagues you? Fear, worry, betrayal, sadness, loneliness? Something else?

What place or season in your past do you wish you could revisit? Why?

How is your life different today because you left behind a place, person, or emotion?

Give Us a King!

LEARN

The first five books of the Bible written by Moses and delineated by genre as the Law give way to a natural curiosity about the history of this Israelite nation. We have already learned much about them in the books of Joshua and Judges, but now we move into the late tenth century BC. Repeatedly in the book of Judges, the author wrote, "In those days Israel had no king." The book of 1 Samuel is a critical turning point in Israel's history. The people will no longer be ruled by judges; they will have a king. God's plan was for Him to be their King, but the rebellious people demanded an earthly king.

There is much controversy about the authorship of both 1 and 2 Samuel. The book's namesake is the prophet Samuel, who was a strong spiritual leader of Israel. First Samuel covers an entire century of history from Samuel's birth to Saul's death.

We will read that Saul was the first king of Israel. He, Samuel, and David will be the focus of this book.

READ

Day One	1 Samuel 1–3
Day Two	1 Samuel 4–7
Day Three	1 Samuel 8–10
Day Four	1 Samuel 11–15
Day Five	1 Samuel 16–20
Day Six	1 Samuel 21–25
Day Seven	1 Samuel 26–31

CONSIDER

In thirty-one chapters we read a massive amount of Israel's history. A record familiar and well-known to the Christian. We've all longed to hear our name in the dead of night and whispered, "Speak, LORD, for your servant is listening" (1 Samuel 3:9 NIV). And, to our detriment, we have desired a king other than the one who longs to be King of our life.

The desire among the Israelites—and among us—to have an earthly leader is not sin. The issue is one of the heart. As we read through Judges, the fact that Israel had no king seems to stand out. The writer is not suggesting that they needed a king; his point is they didn't acknowledge their God as King. It was their obsession with everything else that labeled them as a country with no moral or ethical leadership. Not surprisingly, they continued this practice into the book of 1 Samuel.

The Israelites wanted a king, they wanted what they wanted, and they wanted it now. Like immature little children who can't see past their immediate gratification. The people demanded to be like other countries surrounding them. They demanded to have a human king lead them. They were, in essence, rejecting the God who had been a pillar of fire by night and a cloud by day. This was in direct conflict to the laws they had been given in Moses' writings. Samuel, after inquiring of the Lord, came back to tell them what it would mean to have a king. *The Living Bible* says he told them they would "shed bitter tears" (1 Samuel 8:18 TLB). They wouldn't listen. A shouting mob defying their godly leader called out for a king. You've already read the rest of that story. We will read more history on how that's workin' for them.

We, too, are much like the children of Israel. We look to our government, our church, our family, our friends to fulfill the needs of our lives. We read the advice of famous authors and listen to the speech of life coaches. We watch actors, actresses, and talk show hosts give us instructions on how to live. We click on every link on social media and listen to the instruction of men and women we've never heard of before. We give up friendships with those who disagree with us. We argue with strangers on the internet. We have ignored that we already have a true King, one who sacrificed for our future. We need no other king.

RESPOND

How would you equate our political climate with that of Israel in 1 Samuel?

How do the kings' rights in 1 Samuel 8:1–18 compare with those of our government?

Compare David and Saul's relationship with those among candidates in our elections.

Worship

LEARN

This week we resume our probe into Deuteronomy. We will be instructed in God's commands regarding worship, false prophets, feasts, leaders, and the sabbatical year. Jesus quoted the book of Deuteronomy more often than any other Old Testament book. We will see that he valued the law and learn that He did not come to abolish it.

After the heaviness of Deuteronomy, it's refreshing to hear a few lyrical poems with the promise of redemption. In the second book of the Psalms, the theme is the redemption of man. Written mainly by David, the psalms are emotional and personal. Psalms 42, 47, and 48 have been called "mini hymnals" of God as King.

Persist through Deuteronomy and rejoice through the Psalms. As you read Psalm 42–63, note the words of praise and worship.

READ

CONSIDER

Worship is defined by Dictionary.com as "the feeling or expression of reverence and adoration for a deity." The children of Israel were given explicit rules and regulations concerning how they were to worship in the promised land. Deuteronomy 12 contains these commands. First and foremost, they were to destroy every altar and building, any semblance of the idolatry of other nations. In this new land, they would be shown where to establish the house of the Lord for their worship. They were cautioned not to sacrifice anywhere but in this one place and never to neglect the Levites. The Levites were their spiritual leaders. Moses strongly demanded that they keep their promises to God and never become ensnared by the gods of other nations.

Worship in our culture seems to mean the time in our church service with lights, smoke, a band, singers, and loud music, or a variation thereof. That would not seem to define Israel's worship. Israel's worship was regulated with specific rules as to sacrifices, gatherings, even food. There was a mandated year for debt canceling and the freeing of servants. Through it all, they were reminded to watch out for false prophets who told them what they wanted to hear. Amazingly, God, the creator, defined worship well before Dictionary.com. The Psalms we read this week are indeed worship.

The first verse we read expresses a longing for the living God. In this week's readings the psalmist will praise Him over and over, promising to praise His name. He repeats statements such as that the throne of God will last forever. Salvation comes from God. Great is our Lord and greatly to be praised. The psalmist knew the definition of worship. Do we?

RESPOND

From Deuteronomy 12, which of the rules of worship speak to your heart? Do you practice it today?

Psalm 54:4 refers to God as " the one who sustains me." What does that mean to you?

By pen or in your mind, choose a verse from the weekly reading and rewrite it in your own words.

Frenemies

LEARN

This week we return to Job and his so-called friends and the continuation of his woes. The first eight chapters are Job's continued defense of himself. He addresses both his friends and God. Finally, in chapter 32, a new voice and friend appears. Enter Elihu. Some scholars believe Elihu came upon the scene sometime after the other three. Others believe he was there all the time, as verses 6–9 in chapter 32 explain. Elihu was young, and his claim is that he kept silent until now in honor of the elder and wiser. Elihu has praise for God and honors Him with his words. When God begins to speak, in chapters 38–41, He does not mention Elihu, but He does correct the others.

We will read the end of the story in chapter 42 with Job's final response to God. One in which he repents of his words, accepts God's authority, and experiences renewed confidence in God. Consider Elihu's words carefully as you read chapters 32–37.

READ

Day One	Job 29–31
Day Two	Job 32–33
Day Three	Job 34–35
Day Four	Job 36–37
Day Five	Job 38–39
Day Six	Job 40–41
Day Seven	Job 42

CONSIDER

Throughout the entire book, Job has passionately maintained his innocence. He would not admit any guilt; he believes God has unjustly and wrongly afflicted him. His friends cannot convince him any different. Job ends his tirade against God by stating definitively, "The words of Job are ended" (Job 31:40 NIV). His friends are silenced but do not seem convinced of his purity. These friends who came as comforters have an agenda. They want to be the authority in Job's situation. Even among themselves, they argue about why this has been happening to Job. In another illustration of failing friendship, they give up. Job 32:1 (NIV) says, "So these three men stopped answering Job." Imagine them rolling their eyes, shaking their heads, shrugging, throwing their hands in the air. On the other hand, Elihu has been sitting quietly waiting for his chance. Maybe not even really listening. Elihu has been forming his own argument while the others and Job were speaking, which is evident in that he paraphrases what he heard, telling them, "But you have said in my hearing" (Job 33:8 NIV). Elihu has heard the arguments of the other three and Job's words of defense. Elihu's comments suggest that God is detached from us, that our sin doesn't affect God at all.

Elihu is the friend who listens with a plan to refute what you say. In a disagreement, he isn't listening with an open mind; he's gearing up for his turn. When we don't listen to one another, we do what Elihu did: we misquote and misunderstand the other person's reasoning. As Matthew Henry comments, "Seldom is a quarrel begun, more seldom is a quarrel carried on, in which there are not faults on both sides."[10]

God has had enough of them all. When he begins speaking, in chapters 38–41, he speaks out of a "tempest"—in other words, a storm that has been brewing for a while. God has been listening since the beginning of Job's tribulations and conversations with his friends, and He has heard himself misquoted, misrepresented, and maligned. God has lots of questions that He directs only to Job. The challenge from God that wraps it all up is this: Prove it, prove I've done something wrong. Job, of course, cannot. He does the only thing one can do when God challenges us: repent. It is then, we can say with Job, "I had only heard about you before, but now I have seen you with my own eyes" (Job 42:5 NLT).

RESPOND

What did you see in Elihu's words that rang true for you regarding crisis situations?

What part of God's response did you need to hear? Why?

How do you reconcile Job's restored fortunes with a time you or your friend did not receive restoration?

True or False

LEARN

Jeremiah reappears this week, and we join him in his continued warnings to the nation of Judah. We will finish with his book, but it will be a short reprieve. The major Old Testament prophets were not known for their uplifting messages. These prophecies were harsh, difficult to hear, and well deserved. We have much to learn from their words.

Jeremiah continues his prophetic judgments with words regarding sin, wicked kings, false prophets, and the coming captivity. He is lonely, ostracized, and sad. We will read of his persecutions and his faithfulness to his call. At the end of this week, we will learn of specific nations and their future.

Throughout the book of Jeremiah, we learn of inescapable judgment for an unrepentant nation. Sadly, the unrepentant nations of today's world will not escape either.

READ

Day One	Jeremiah 15-17
Day Two	Jeremiah 18-24
Day Three	Jeremiah 25-29
Day Four	Jeremiah 30-35
Day Five	Jeremiah 36-40
Day Six	Jeremiah 41-46
Day Seven	Jeremiah 47-52

CONSIDER

This entire book is one big warning and disaster proclamation. Nobody wants to hear these kinds of prophecies, but these people had been brutal in their persecution of Jeremiah. They "attacked" him with their tongues, ignored what he said, and spread rumors about him. He was beaten, put in prison, thrown in a cistern. He had to deal with liars and deceivers daily. It's no wonder he had his moments of self-pity: "It's for your sake that I am suffering" (Jeremiah 15:15 NLT). In other words, nobody will help me, and I never get to go to a party. In a final blow, King Jehoiakim takes Jeremiah's written prophecies, cuts them in pieces, and throws them into a fire pit. How could one not believe Jeremiah's words? The true test of a prophecy is whether it happens or not. Jeremiah's predictions transpire all throughout this book.

What of today? In our world, prophecy is a little known entity and prophets are without honor. In some ways, rightly so. So many men and women have claimed to be prophets and publicized their "word from God." Some of them have done so for fame and fortune. Some of them have exploited God's people. What should be our response? Do we accept or deny those words called prophetic? Do we disregard self-proclaimed prophets? Jeremiah gave us the instructions in chapter 28, verse 9 (NLT): "So a prophet who predicts peace must show he is right. Only when his predictions come true can we know that he is really from the LORD." A word from God will always line up with *the* Word of God. Prophecies are only prophetic if they come to pass.

RESPOND

What do you know and believe about prophetic words?

Have you heard a "prophecy" that did not come true? How did that affect your belief about prophecy?

Have you prophesied to or about a person or situation? What was your first reaction to that question?

Set Free

LEARN

After Jeremiah's tough words, Paul's reprimands seem mild. This week we read about Paul's continued ministry. Paul kept in close contact with the church at Corinth, as seen in 1 Corinthians. After that first letter, the church continued to have issues, so Paul traveled to meet with them in person. It was not a vacation. Scholars report that the visit was painful for Paul and the church. He was returning to Rome through Macedonia. He learned that the Corinthians were still infighting, so he wrote this second letter. He addresses three groups in the church: the faithful majority, the easily influenced minority, and the false teachers themselves.

At the end of the week, we will read Paul's relatively short letter to the Galatians. This letter was written in 49 AD, before the letters to Corinth, and was probably the first letter he wrote. The church at Galatia was in conflict over salvation. Some Jewish teachers of the law were confusing the new converts with the law of Moses and the gospel of grace. They needed victory over legalism. The letter indicates that these teachers were personally attacking Paul because he wasn't an original disciple. Never one to back down, Paul addresses the charges in this letter.

READ

Day One	2 Corinthians 1-3
Day Two	2 Corinthians 4-5
Day Three	2 Corinthians 6-8
Day Four	2 Corinthians 9-10
Day Five	2 Corinthians 11-13
Day Six	Galatians 1-3
Day Seven	Galatians 4-6

CONSIDER

This week's reading contains some of the richest and well-known scripture in the New Testament. Paul's second letter to Corinth is another example of his great love for the church. This love compels him to instruct them and discipline them. It is in this book that we learn to comfort one another with the comfort we have been given. Herein are principles to discipline our brothers and sisters within the church. We discover the treasure inside our bodies of clay. We're encouraged to be generous. We obtain weapons for warfare that are not worldly. We realize that our thoughts govern our behavior and emotions. We must take control of our thoughts. We are assured that His grace is adequate for all situations.

If that were not enough to encourage us in the Christian walk, Paul gives us the letter to Galatia and declares our freedom. Freedom from sin also affords us the freedom to be who God calls us to be. It frees us from unreasonable expectations, whether from others or ourselves. It frees us to acknowledge our weaknesses, to grieve as well as to celebrate. In her book *You Are Free: Be Who You Already Are*, Rebekah Lyons says, "Freedom comes when we know God is enough."[11]

To be sure, both of these churches had their difficulties, and Paul addresses those. The church at Galatia were adamant about the law. Some of this body of believers were confusing truth with false teachings. Even so Paul calls these people the "only letter of recommendation" he needs: "The only letter of recommendation we need is you yourselves. Your lives are a letter written in our hearts; everyone can read it and recognize our good work among you. Clearly, you are a letter from Christ showing the result of our ministry among you. This 'letter' is written not with pen and ink, but with the Spirit of the living God. It is carved not on tablets of stone, but on human hearts" (2 Corinthians 3:2–3 NLT). The Galatians were the example of Paul's teachings. Their lives were the result of his work among them. His reference to the ten commandments written in stone suggests that they had embraced these laws and believed them in their hearts.

RESPOND

How do you define freedom in Christ?

Can your spiritual leaders say 2 Corinthians 3:2–3 about you? Why or why not?

Who is your "letter of recommendation" and why?

Changed in the Twinkling of an Eye

LEARN

Luke is the only non-Jewish writer of any book in the Bible. His Gospel and the book of Acts comprise over one fourth of the New Testament. His lengthy writing focuses on Jesus' many parables and teaching but does not neglect the reporting of miracles. Luke emphasized that salvation was for everyone, an appropriate teaching for his audience of Gentiles. He most frequently refers to Jesus as the "Son of Man" and attributes great importance to the Holy Spirit. His comprehensive Gospel includes Jesus' concern for the marginalized. Luke likely gathered his information from a variety of sources. Many of those would have been eyewitness accounts.

When we last left Luke, Jesus was beginning his ministry in Galilee. Our reading will continue with that record. Luke, like all the other Gospel writers, will record Peter's confession of Christ, the confession upon which the church will be built. He will report many of the same narratives as the other Gospel writers, but with more detail. Luke's Gospel immediately takes us on the final journey toward Jerusalem and into Jesus' final week on Earth.

For those of us who know these stories well, they are easily taken for granted. Take a breath; these words were written for you.

READ

Day One	Luke 9-11
Day Two	Luke 12-14
Day Three	Luke 15-17
Day Four	Luke 18-19
Day Five	Luke 20
Day Six	Luke 21-22
Day Seven	Luke 23-24

CONSIDER

Three of the four Gospel writers include an account of Jesus being "transfigured." It's a brief interlude. John alludes to it in the introduction to his Gospel: "We have seen his glory" (John 1:14 NIV). Luke affords the event seven verses: Luke 9:28–35.

Jesus had told his disciples that he would die. It was about a week later when he took Peter, James, and John onto a mountain to pray. Luke has been meticulous in recording Jesus' emphasis on prayer. It is no surprise that he reported this event with detail. While Jesus was praying, "the appearance of his face changed, and his clothes became as bright as a flash of lightning" (Luke 9:29 NIV).

"His face changed." No one records exactly how, but we do know He was in prayer, in conversation with His Father. His Father may have been encouraging Him about what was ahead. Or perhaps, simply being in the presence of His father changed His countenance.

"His clothes became as bright as a flash of lightening." Matthew's version says, "white as light" (Matthew 17:2 NLT), and practical Mark writes, "His clothes became dazzling white, whiter than anyone in the world could bleach them" (Mark 9:3 NIV).

The event was for the disciples who witnessed it. It was revelatory, prophetic, and instructional. The change in Jesus' face and clothing as he talked with Moses and Elijah revealed his oneness with God. That they were on Earth to talk with Jesus was a picture of eternal life. It revealed that Jesus truly was God in the flesh. The voice from inside the cloud instructed the three disciples to "listen to him" (Luke 9:35 NIV).

For us, it is a lesson in prayer. We are changed physically and emotionally when we spend time with our Heavenly Father, listening as well as petitioning. Relationships are built by spending time with someone. Talking and listening, sharing emotions, situations, experiences. We build a relationship with God in the same way. Our faces should be changed when we are with Him. Our clothes will be changed when we transition to heaven.

RESPOND

What do you understand about the transfiguration?

What, if any, changes do you see in your life when you commune with God?

Why do you suppose eyewitness John doesn't mention the transfiguration?

Boldly Approach the Throne

LEARN

This week we languish again in the desert where the Israelites are wandering and resume the reading of Moses' laws. These last chapters deal with the worship of Yahweh. The instructions include constructing the tabernacle and its furnishings, the garments and consecration of the priests. Once again, there are warnings about idolatry, a familiar theme for these people.

We read in chapter 24 about the confirmation of God's covenant with the people of Israel. Immediately following, God provided specific instructions about his tabernacle and the items to be placed inside. He included exact dimensions and materials as well. From chapter 25 to chapter 31, we will read of these precise instructions. While Moses labors on the mountain to understand and record these plans, the children of Israel get restless. They decide Moses has disappeared forever, and they need to make their own way through this wilderness. So they throw all their jewelry in a pot, melt it down, and make a golden calf. Then the people say, "These are your gods who brought you out of the land of Egypt" (Exodus 32:4 NLT). It seems unimaginable.

God tells Moses to get down there because his people "have been quick to turn away" (Exodus 32:8 NIV). We'll read all about it and what happens after. Then we will read again the instructions about the tabernacle. Moses had to rewrite God's words after the calf incident. Don't be too quick to judge these people; Gentile Christians do their share of not listening too. Listen as you read.

READ

Day One	Exodus 25–27
Day Two	Exodus 28–29
Day Three	Exodus 30–31
Day Four	Exodus 32–34
Day Five	Exodus 35–37
Day Six	Exodus 38–39
Day Seven	Exodus 40

CONSIDER

The tabernacle of the Old Testament and its fixtures are an interesting study. Each piece is significant in its own right. The dimensions of the pieces were not chosen because God is a control freak; there were natural reasons for each piece. There was purpose in each object's placement. The tabernacle itself was constructed for community and worship. Much is written and has been spoken of about these furnishings, but let's take a look at the one significant item mentioned later, in a most important tale.

In Exodus 25, God told Moses to have the people bring offerings of metals, wood, and fabric. He asked for them to give what their heart told them to. Think about that for a minute. Give what your heart tells you to.

The people gave blue, purple, scarlet yarn and fine linen, goat hair, ram skins dyed red, and hides of sea cows (similar to manatees). From this they made curtains, but one was made differently: "Then he made another curtain for the entrance to the sacred tent. He made it of finely woven linen and embroidered it with exquisite designs using blue, purple, and scarlet thread. This curtain was hung on gold hooks attached to five posts. The posts with their decorated tops and hooks were overlaid with gold, and the five bases were cast from bronze" (Exodus 36:37–38 NLT). The curtain was fifteen feet high and fifteen feet wide. This curtain separated the *most* holy place from the holy place. Inside the most Holy Place was the ark of the covenant. This was the place where God resided. Only the high priest could go through that curtain and only once or twice a year. God could only be approached by a certain person and only after a long list of rules and regulations were met.

Matthew, Mark, and Luke make an interesting comment about this curtain in one verse with no elaboration. "And the curtain in the sanctuary of the Temple was torn in two, from top to bottom" (Mark 15:38 NLT; also see Luke 23:45 and Matthew 27:51). That fifteen-foot-high curtain woven tightly was ripped from top to bottom as Jesus died on the cross. The curtain that for thousands of years had separated humanity from God was gone.

RESPOND

Which of the tabernacle furnishings do you find the most interesting? Why?

Why do you think God was so specific in His instructions?

What is your first reaction to the torn curtain of the tabernacle?

Get Smart

LEARN

The books of history and law in the Old Testament are so intertwined, they are hard to distinguish. Each of them has a little of both genres included. This week we are going to read 2 Samuel and Solomon's proverbs. In the original Hebrew Bible, 1 and 2 Samuel were one book. Samuel was a contributor to the first book, but the main author of both is anonymous. Second Samuel continues the story of the reign of David, beginning after Saul's death. King David is the most well-known king of Israel, and his stories are the most reported in the Old Testament. Much of 2 Samuel will be repeated in 2 Chronicles. Those of us who know the story well should read this book in a different translation than we're used to and search for new meaning among the familiar words, especially chapter 7 and its teaching about covenants.

Throughout the written accounts of history, Solomon ut-
tered over three thousand wise sayings. The history of Israel documents his wisdom. Tradition refers to him as the wisest man
ever to live. About eight hundred of his sayings are gathered in
the book of Proverbs. The words of the book are inspired wisdom. It is simply a book of guidance, not necessarily commands
or promises. Of the ten chapters we will read this week, the first
nine are addressed to Solomon's son. They give him advice to
act properly no matter the situation. The tenth begins a series of
seemingly random one-sentence lessons. Son, daughter, parent,
or aged, these words are good counsel for everyone.

READ

Day One	2 Samuel 1–4
Day Two	2 Samuel 5–9
Day Three	2 Samuel 10–14
Day Four	2 Samuel 15–19
Day Five	2 Samuel 20–24
Day Six	Proverbs 1–5
Day Seven	Proverbs 6–10

CONSIDER

Second Samuel records King David's victories over other
kings and nations. He was a victorious, mighty warrior. His story is well-known among Christians.

Solomon's entire book of Proverbs gives practical wisdom on living. The first nine chapters have a personal slant. In the first few verses, Solomon gives his mission for this missive (Proverbs 1:2–7), explaining that these words will teach wisdom and restraint in our behavior. If followed, these warnings will lead to a successful life. This is a book for everyone; the wise will become even more wise, and everyone can use the instruction. In Proverbs 1:4, he refers to the simple. Note that "simple" here means those who are open to instruction.

Our world interprets "simple" as those who are not quite as intelligent as the rest of the world. Solomon, however, intends it to be a compliment. Those who are open to wisdom, discipline, and instruction will be great. Give me a simple leader any day.

RESPOND

Which of these do you identify with and why? (You can pick more than one.)

- Disciplined
- Successful
- Wise
- Simple
- Just

How does the book of Proverbs relate to you based on your answer above?

Choose a proverb from this week's reading and consider how it could apply to your current situation.

Redeemed

LEARN

The chapters of Deuteronomy for this week may seem harsh and reference "evil" frequently. The writer demands the evil to be purged from the people. There are many if-then statements: if you do this, then this will happen. Some are positive, but most are warnings against bad behavior. Much of the book is repetitious from other books of the Law previously recorded. These laws were to be taken seriously and followed explicitly. Apparently, they had to be repeated often for the benefit of people who seemingly had ears but did not listen.

As always, it's a relief to infuse these strict laws with the psalms of redemption. Psalms 64–72 continue to proclaim gratitude for the redemption of our souls. Psalms 73–83 are songs of God and man, while Psalm 78 could be the national anthem of Judah. Sprinkle the Psalms reading throughout your week and be refreshed.

READ

CONSIDER

The words of Moses in Deuteronomy 26:16–19 were a covenant with the children of Israel. A covenant that contained an important aforementioned if-then statement. Three times in the first three verses (16–18), Moses uses the word *obey*. In verse 19 (NLT), he says, "And if you do, . . . praise, honor, renown" and becoming a nation "holy to the LORD" would be the reward.

Thousands of years after Moses would write Deuteronomy 26:16–19, Paul would affirm, "For all of God's promises have been fulfilled in Christ with a resounding 'Yes!' And through Christ, our 'Amen' (which means 'Yes') ascends to God for his glory" (2 Corinthians 1:20 NLT).

Why is it so difficult to obey? Is it for lack of listening? There is a difference between hearing and listening. Hearing is sounds swirling around us with little notice. There's a plane flying overhead right now, and the maintenance men have been shoveling snow and scraping the pavement all morning. The dog upstairs is running through the house pounding the ceiling. None of this is distracting. Listening is different. Listening requires paying attention and understanding the intent of the message. Moses had been giving (and we have been reading) a multitude of rules and regulations. It's easy to doze off or slip into a daydream.

But in Psalm 81:8 (NLT) God begs us to listen: "Listen to me, oh my people, while I give you stern warnings. O, Israel if you would only listen to me." Most translations say "listen," but the CEV says "pay attention." The Hebrew word used here means "to hear intelligently." If one hears with intelligence, he or she will grasp the "stern warnings." Throughout the history of the Israelites, God laments again and again that the people would not listen.

Mark Twain said, "If you were supposed to talk more than you listen, you'd have two mouths and one ear." Perhaps that's why God created us this way.

RESPOND

Compare listening with obeying in your own life.

Pinpoint an if-then statement you have heard from God in your lifetime.

What does Paul mean when he says God's promises have been fulfilled in Christ?

Right and Wrong

LEARN

This week gives us an opportunity to review history through 1 Chronicles and gather some wisdom from Solomon. Chronicles may have been written by Ezra, but no one is sure. The book was written to the exiles who have returned to their homeland but are still ruled by the kings of Persia. The author hopes to encourage them by reiterating their illustrious history. Chronicles begins with nine chapters of genealogy. A bit of a snooze fest but important in reminding these people (and us) from whence they came. It is repetitious in many areas but adds more detail to David's exploits. Chronicles will be a break from the woe of the prophecies, as it focuses on positive events. It was written to encourage. There will be no mention of David's sin or the wicked kings of the northern kingdom, Israel. It begins with Saul's death and ends with David's last words. This history will be interspersed with more of Solomon's wise words from Proverbs as well.

READ

Day One	1 Chronicles 1-4
Day Two	1 Chronicles 5-9
Day Three	1 Chronicles 10-14
Day Four	Proverbs 11-15
Day Five	1 Chronicles 15-19
Day Six	Proverbs 16-21
Day Seven	1 Chronicles 20-24

CONSIDER

The readings this week in 1 Chronicles provide additional proof of previous scripture. The added content which never contradicts another writing adds accuracy to the original historical account. Chapters 1–9 trace lineage from Adam forward, though the majority of recorded genealogies do not go back to the beginning of man. It is helpful to remember that Chronicles overlaps with the books of Samuel and Kings; thus there is an abundance of parallel information. Nevertheless, there is purpose in all of these writings.

Let's look at Solomon's own writings and consider whether the advice of Proverbs 11–21 mirrored his father's example.

Proverbs 12:1, 14:29, 17:27, and 21:1 give various suggestions on how to follow God's ways. Proverbs 12:1 (NLT) is particularly explicit with the statement, "It is stupid to hate correction." Following the Hebrew, the word *stupid* means "brutish," which is defined as "cruel and violent." Solomon, like his father, knew he could not rule effectively without knowing God.

Solomon's purpose was to build the temple, but the wise man knew and followed his wisdom: "Commit your actions to the LORD, and your plans will succeed" (Proverbs 16:3 NLT). He also cautioned, "Plans go wrong for lack of advice; many advisers bring success" (Proverbs 15:22 NLT).

To address right and wrong, the Proverbs are extensive in wisdom. See Proverbs 11:19, 13:5, 14:12, and 15:29. The entire Bible is a promise and a warning regarding the good sense in choosing right over wrong.

RESPOND

How far can you trace your genealogy, and what do you find there?

What do you suppose was the purpose for the parallel information in 1 Chronicles?

What is an example from your life when plans went "wrong for lack of advice"?

Observe, Inquire, Inform

LEARN

When one googles *prophecy*, the first hit is the definition with an example: "a prediction. A bleak prophecy of war and ruin." This definition writer must have been thinking of the prophecy books of the Old Testament. These men, justifiably, had little good news in their prophecies. In fact, the only good news was their own faith and trust in the almighty God.

Lamentations is a short book of grief-filled poems written by Jeremiah as he was carried off into captivity with the rest of the Jews at Jerusalem. He is no longer giving warnings; he is in mourning for his homeland and his people. He is lamenting. He writes five poems, the first four in Acrostic, the first letter of each verse in alphabetical Hebrew. If the book of Jeremiah was the cause, Lamentations is the effect.

Ezekiel was only twenty-five years old when exiled from his homeland. His ministry encompasses the worst hours of Old

Testament history: seven years before the complete destruction of Jerusalem and the fifteen years following. As a contemporary of Jeremiah, he was doubtless influenced by Jeremiah's writings. In the first chapter, he records his call. Most Bible scholars consider Ezekiel's writings the most difficult to understand. He was described as "eccentric, bizarre, and outrageous."[12] Landon MacDonald calls him the "performance art prophet."[13] The imagery used in this book is difficult even for those who are Star Wars or Harry Potter fans. Nevertheless, Ezekiel had an inspired message, and God placed it in the Bible for our instruction. Jabe Nicholson calls it tedious but suggests that we not choke on the bones, just enjoy what we can.[14]

READ

Day One	Lamentations
Day Two	Ezekiel 1–4
Day Three	Ezekiel 5–8
Day Four	Ezekiel 9–12
Day Five	Ezekiel 13–16
Day Six	Ezekiel 17–20
Day Seven	Ezekiel 21–24

CONSIDER

Jeremiah's grief-filled poems follow a timeline in the book of Lamentations. First, he writes sadly about Jerusalem, the location of the Israelites' home. Second, he writes of their punishment. God has handed them over without pity. And they deserved it. He indulges in self-pity in chapter 3. In chapter 4 he records the heartbreak and hardship as the people trudge out of the city. In chapter 5 he prays for their return but knows it will take seventy years.

Amid this book of sorrows, Jeremiah cannot help but remember what he knows about his God, proclaiming, "Yet I still dare to hope" (Lamentations 3:21 NLT). He enumerates what he has experienced in his walk with God: His faithful love never ends, His mercies never cease, His faithfulness is great, the Lord is good to those who depend on Him. Because of this, it's okay to wait for the Lord to act. "For no one is abandoned by the Lord forever. Though he brings grief, he also shows compassion because of the greatness of his unfailing love. For he does not enjoy hurting people or causing them sorrow" (Lamentations 3:31–33 NLT).

To *know* means "to be aware of through observation, inquiry or information." Jeremiah had observed God's work, he frequently inquired of the Lord, and God had given him divine information. Thus far in our reading, Moses, David, Solomon, Paul, and Jesus have urged us to "know" God. Jeremiah further implies we can't get through life without observing, asking, and listening, all of which are vital for knowing God.

RESPOND

What is the purpose of observing the work of the Lord?

How would you respond to exile?

What do you still dare to hope for?

Sacred Mailmen

LEARN

Paul's writings again follow the element of a letter. They begin with a greeting. The body contains gratitude, clarification, and counsel. It ends with an appropriate closing usually with Paul's handwritten signature. Each of his letters were personal and written with different purposes according to the church's need. The three letters to be read this week are to churches that were not in need of discipline as Corinth was. These churches were healthy and effective. It is likely that when a specific church finished with Paul's letter, it was passed on to other churches in the area. Ephesians 1:1 (NLT) says, "This letter is from Paul, chosen by the will of God to be an apostle of Christ Jesus. I am writing to God's holy people in Ephesus, who are faithful followers of Christ Jesus." Some scholars believe the churches inserted their own name in this verse before sharing with their assembly. "I am writing to God's holy people in Denver." True or not, Paul's messages were relevant to the churches then and now.

The history of the church at Ephesus is recorded in Acts 18 and 19. Paul cofounded the church with Priscilla and Aquilla of Acts fame. In 62 AD Paul wrote this letter from a Roman prison. He encouraged the church to grow, not in number but in faith. Chapters 1–3 concentrate on what it means to be "in" Christ, and chapters 4–6 focus on what is done "through" Christ. Paul's coworker Tychicus was given the task of hand-delivering this letter to the church.

Tychicus was also given the letter to the church at Colossae, a church Paul had never visited. The two letters resemble each other in content. Epaphras probably founded the Colossian church after being converted by Paul at Ephesus. After some time, Epaphras went to Rome to ask Paul for his help. False teachers had infiltrated the church. Epaphras needed help in refuting them. Paul's letter to Ephesus involves more advice than discipline. He encourages them to be victorious over heresy.

The Philippian church began during Paul's second missionary journey recorded in Acts 16. When this church found out Paul was imprisoned, they sent a representative, Epaphroditus, to Rome. He was to give financial and emotional support to their imprisoned leader. This letter was Paul's response, a letter of gratitude sent back with Epaphroditus. Read Paul's letters carefully, looking for applicability to your own life.

READ

Day One	Ephesians 1–2
Day Two	Ephesians 3–4
Day Three	Ephesians 5–6
Day Four	Colossians 1–2
Day Five	Colossians 3–4
Day Six	Philippians 1–2
Day Seven	Philippians 3–4

CONSIDER

In none of these letters does Paul express any remorse or sadness about his situation. When he writes a few verses of discipline, they are kind and relaxed. The first ten verses of Ephesians don't even mention that he is writing from prison. Instead, he writes an inventory of gratitude to God. He says much the same to the Colossians. The first chapter is gratitude for their devotion to God. In his letter to the Philippians, he uses the word "joy" in the fourth verse. He writes the word "joy" fifteen more times in the letter.

Joy, Paul had joy. Think about where he is and what he is facing. Joy is not a feeling we would equate with Paul's condition. Maybe it's not a feeling you can equate with your present.

Joy is not the same as happiness. Joy is the surprise. The shock of a smile when you've got nothing to smile about. The good night's sleep when you've got plenty to keep you awake. The contentment when everything crashes around you. The unexplainable, absolute assurance that your outcome is not dependent on you. Circumstances do not steal joy.

Paul knew that; he wanted the churches of the New Testament to know that. He wanted the churches of today to know it.

RESPOND

How did these churches differ in their need of instruction?

Which of the three messengers—Tychicus, Epaphras, or Epaphroditus—do you identify with most? Why?

List examples of joy and happiness from your life.

Come and See

LEARN

John, the beloved disciple. One of the first disciples called. Part of Jesus' inner circle. A fisherman by trade. The author with the most to say wrote his account of the gospel almost twenty years after the others. Ancient sources indicate an elderly John, living in Ephesus, was asked to write his account of Jesus Christ, presumably to refute a false narrative that was being circulated. John immediately makes clear that Jesus "was with God in the beginning" (John 1:2 NIV) and calls Him "the Word [who] became flesh" (John 1:14 NIV). If you are only going to read and study one book in the entire Bible, John's Gospel is the recommendation. For those who are questioning salvation or the newly saved, this is the book for reference. For these reasons, we read only the first half of the book this week. Savor it.

READ

CONSIDER

John was Jesus' beloved friend. His writings show that the feeling was mutual. John's apparent hesitation to write about his friend reminds me of Luke's words about Mary: "Mary kept all these things in her heart and thought about them often" (Luke 2:19 NLT).

John's book has a tone of love, respect, and awe that can only be felt by one who has been with Jesus. John shares some but not all of the miracles he witnessed. John extensively quotes Jesus. His writings testify that he knew Old Testament scripture well. John is the only disciple who records Jesus' conversation with Nicodemus, a conversation that sums up the entire gospel message.

Throughout the Bible the words "come and see" can be found 836 times. John records them twice in the first chapter.

In verse 39 Jesus tells two of John the Baptist's disciples to "come and see," and in verse 46 Phillip invites Nathaniel to check Jesus out for himself. "Come and see." But in John 4:29, John's recording of this phrase is the beginning of Jesus' public ministry on Earth. A familiar story of the Samaritan woman at the well.

This woman was unworthy and unclean in the eyes of everyone who beheld her. A woman with a reputation for adultery, immorality, and self-indulgence. People turned the other way when she appeared, shunned by her family and former friends. When this woman shouted, "Come and see," in the streets, people ran to see. Jesus stayed there for two more days, and many believed His message because they came to see. They came to investigate for themselves the things they were hearing about Jesus.

John's gospel invites us to come and see. You have come with your commitment to read the Bible through this year; don't fail now to open your eyes wide and see.

RESPOND

What did you see in this week's reading that challenged you?

Why do you suppose the people listened to the Samaritan women's invitation?

How would you invite someone to "come and see"? Whom should you invite?

Return to the Law

LEARN

The book of Leviticus was written by Moses in 1445–1405 BC. It takes its name from the priestly tribe of Levi. Leviticus is a true book of laws, covering everything from worship to food and clothing practices. Controversial in our world today, its explicit and descriptive language is often disgusting. Technically and according to Scripture, the relationship of man with God before Jesus was dependent on sacrifice. Fellowship with God was dependent on separation from sin. This book outlines the smallest details of sacrifice and regulations. It was and is a guidebook to holiness. The first sixteen chapters point the way to God, the only way to God before Christ.

In reading, it may be difficult to see its relevance to today. Its emphasis on atonement, blood sacrifice, and holiness are important to believers as it was "a shadow, a dim preview of the good things to come" (Hebrews 10:1 NLT). The old system under the Law of Moses was this shadow. The sacrifices under that system were repeated again and again, year after year, but they were never able to provide perfect cleansing for those who came to worship. Read with a heart of gratitude for the supreme sacrifice.

READ

Day One	Leviticus 1–3
Day Two	Leviticus 4–5
Day Three	Leviticus 6–8
Day Four	Leviticus 9–11
Day Five	Leviticus 12–13
Day Six	Leviticus 14–15
Day Seven	Leviticus 16–17

CONSIDER

If nothing else came from this week's reading, one can be grateful that we no longer live under these old laws. It's unnecessary to hold a squirming animal and lean into it while it is slaughtered, blood and guts spraying over you. Thank you, Jesus. We no longer need a priest or mediator to speak for us at the throne. Jesus' final sacrifice gave us complete access to the Father and to heaven.

The book of Leviticus is written as legislation. Its structure resembles that of a legal document with verses and verses of stated law. Between the decrees of chapter 9 and 11, Moses diverts to twenty narrative verses. He relates the story of his two nephews, two of the sons of his brother, Aaron. This family of priests had been given strict rules about their behavior. The first two verses state the facts. The priests were holy to God; they had strict orders in the performance of their duties. These two didn't take their positions seriously. They did what they wanted with little regard for the laws of God. God was making it clear that his laws could not be violated without punishment.

Moses does not comfort his brother in the death of his sons; instead, he defends God. Leviticus 10:3 (NLT) says, "This is what the LORD meant when he said, 'I will display my holiness through those who come near me. I will display my glory before all the people."

When ministers of God commit obvious sin, the cause of Christ is thwarted. When a man or woman of God fails morally, legally, or spiritually, there is damage to the message of the gospel. These men and women are rarely killed on the spot. But be assured God will always demand punishment for sin.

RESPOND

What was Moses' purpose in the narrative story of the death of Aaron's sons?

Why do you suppose Aaron was silent at Moses' words?

Was there a particular law from that reading that gave you pause? Why?

History Repeats Itself

LEARN

History lovers are in their element this week as we read the entire book of 1 Kings. You can't make this stuff up. In this book are the stories of thirteen kings, their victories and defeats, and their personal lives that boggle the mind. Historical writers have the most interesting characters, settings, and plots for content. 1 Kings is no exception. The author is anonymous. The book is likely a compilation by several authors written in 560–550 BC.

The book was written to confront the exiles with their erratic history. The Israelites had demanded a king when Samuel was their prophet. He had tried to talk them out of it, but they insisted and here's what transpired. The writers of 1 Kings evaluate each king's performance based on his behavior. For the most part, the picture wasn't pretty.

The first eleven chapters chronicle Solomon's reign, including the temple construction. His was not a reign without con-

troversy and sin. Still, God is a God of his word, as promised in
1 Kings 9:5 (NIV): "I will establish your royal throne over Israel
forever, as I promised David your father when I said, 'You shall
never fail to have a successor on the throne of Israel.'" Judah
would always be ruled by a descendant of David. Chapter 12
will explain how Israel came to be a nation divided. The following eleven evaluate the kings from both nations. Even if you are
not a history buff, read thoughtfully, for as Winston Churchill
once said, "Those that fail to learn from history are doomed to
repeat it."

READ

Day One	1 Kings 1-4
Day Two	1 Kings 5-7
Day Three	1 Kings 8-10
Day Four	1 Kings 11-14
Day Five	1 Kings 15-16
Day Six	1 Kings 17-20
Day Seven	1 Kings 21-22

CONSIDER

Solomon, the wisest king ever, caused the split in the people of God. Sometimes, that fact is overlooked. Chapter 11 tells
us that King Solomon liked the ladies. He "loved" many foreign

wives, women from the very nations God had said to stay away from. As he advanced in age, these loves turned his heart from his first love. He was no longer fully devoted to God, and his behavior led to idolatry. Worse, he led others into idolatry. God became angry, as he always does when his people turn to idols. "So now the LORD said to him, 'Since you have not kept my covenant and have disobeyed my decrees, I will surely tear the kingdom away from you and give it to one of your servants. But for the sake of your father, David, I will not do this while you are still alive. I will take the kingdom away from your son. And even so, I will not take away the entire kingdom; I will let him be king of one tribe, for the sake of my servant David and for the sake of Jerusalem, my chosen city" (1 Kings 11:11–13 NLT).

On the surface, one wonders how God differentiated sin in the lives of these two men. Solomon loved the wrong women, but David was an adulterer, murderer, and liar. Both men were sinners. The difference: David never turned to a god of wood and stone. For a moment he let his heart wander to a woman on a rooftop, but he never worshiped her. Solomon, on the other hand, tolerated his wives' false gods until his heart accepted them. He gave his heart to "Ashtoreth the goddess of the Sidonians, and Molek the detestable god of the Ammonites" (1 Kings 11:5 NIV). He even built shrines for the gods of all his wives (1 Kings 11:7–8 NIV). Molech was an idol to whom children were sacrificed under Solomon's reign. Solomon had wandered far from the God of his father.

That is not the wonder of this scripture. "Even so," God says (1 Kings 11:12 TLB). God was a God of His word. What he promises cannot be undone by the sin of people. To be sure, there are consequences for every action, as there were for Solomon's, but God's word is trustworthy. In previous readings we read the covenant made with David that he would always have a successor on the throne. Amid Solomon's sin and idolatry, God could not break that promise.

God was always trying to give David and Solomon a way out. He was determined to keep his promise along with discipline. It is true for us also. In our failures, wickedness, and transgressions, God is always offering forgiveness. Always offering reinstatement, always promising to make good of our mistakes. The only requirement is to put nothing else above Him.

RESPOND

How reassuring is it to know God is always looking for a way to help you out of the mess of your own making?

What could Solomon have done to avoid being led into idolatry?

Which of the kings you read about intrigued you? How could you find out more about him?

Songs in the Desert

LEARN

This week's reading will complete the book of Deuteronomy. Recalling that the Psalms were divided into five books, we will also complete the third and fourth books of the Psalms.

The last four chapters of Deuteronomy record Moses' final words to the people of Israel, his death, and the appointment of Joshua to succeed him. It is a blend of happy and unhappy. Because of sin, Moses was not allowed to enter the promised land, but God allowed him to see it from a mountaintop. He blessed his people and left them with life-giving words. There had never been before and has never been since a prophet like Moses. He is the only one to whom God spoke face-to-face.

The Psalms reading will be reminiscent of the Israelites' time in the desert. Psalms 104–106 are designated the historical psalms. The Psalms could be classified as a "divine hymnal." At any given time, in any given circumstance, one of the Psalms can address your issue. Look for the correlation between Deuteronomy 32 and Psalm 90 in this week's reading.

READ

Day One	Deuteronomy 31-32
Day Two	Deuteronomy 33-34
Day Three	Psalms 84-89
Day Four	Psalms 90-95
Day Five	Psalms 96-100
Day Six	Psalms 101-103
Day Seven	Psalms 104-106

CONSIDER

Imagine the scene: after forty long years of wandering around in circles, the Israelites are standing on the brink of the promised land. Moses knows he will not cross the Jordan; he has been grooming Joshua for the task of leadership for years. They had reached the goal that had been many years in the making.

It's not out of the question that the people sang, "You have restored the fortunes of Jacob" (Psalm 85:1 TLB). We will make known your faithfulness to all generations. Sing to the Lord a new song. Shout for joy to the Lord. Give thanks to the Lord. Praise the Lord. The Psalms that had not yet been written on parchment; they were being sung on the lips of the people.

Moses had given volumes of rules and regulations to make the Israelites successful, but he can't resist one last caution: "These instructions are not empty words—they are your life! By obeying them you will enjoy a long life in the land you will occupy when you cross the Jordan River" (Deuteronomy 32:47 NLT).

Deuteronomy 32 is called the "Song of Moses," written to remind the Israelites that their entire existence was a result of God's faithfulness. Psalm 90 is attributed as a "prayer of Moses, the man of God." Both acknowledge the faithfulness of God throughout "all generations" (Psalm 90:1 NIV).

Psalm 90:12 (NLT) says, "Teach us to realize the brevity of life, so that we may grow in wisdom." Moses prays that we understand the shortness of this life in comparison to eternity. Comprehending the shortness of life should cause us to spend our days thoughtfully. His song of Deuteronomy 32 reminded the Israelites of the past mistakes the people had made while wandering through the wilderness. In Psalm 90 we are reminded that life is short. As we consider this short life, we should also consider the adage, "Learn from the mistakes of others. You won't live long enough to make them all yourself."

RESPOND

Imagine yourself on the brink of the promised land. What do you see? What do you hear? How do you feel?

Perhaps you are on the brink of something in your life: empty nest, new spouse, new baby, new job, cross-country move. What mistakes do you need to avoid in this new undertaking?

What have you learned from the mistakes of others?

Ancient Words

LEARN

Once again, we look at David's reign, this time at the hand-off of the kingdom to Solomon. Much of our historical reading seems repetitious as we trudge through the historical books. Be assured they each have a purpose for the past and the future. Much of the Chronicles reading this week will be an accounting of names and assignments. Second Chronicles will detail the temple preparations and building as well as Solomon's popularity. Ask the Spirit to help you see purpose in it.

READ

Day One   1 Chronicles 25-27
Day Two   1 Chronicles 28-29
Day Three   2 Chronicles 1-4
Day Four   2 Chronicles 5-7

CONSIDER

We have read before that the kingdom handoff from David to Solomon was not easy. First Kings records the difficulties surrounding Solomon's appointment. Solomon's many half brothers caused more than half of David's problems, and these were passed on to Solomon. Even so, David knew that Solomon should be and would be his successor. Oddly, Solomon did not become king due to his father's death. David stepped aside in obedience to God's command and let Solomon take the throne. In 1 Chronicles 28:9 (NLT), David gives his son some prudent advice: "And Solomon, my son, learn to know the God of your ancestors intimately. Worship and serve him with your whole heart and a willing mind. For the LORD sees every heart and knows every plan and thought. If you seek him, you will find him. But if you forsake him, he will reject you forever." Four phrases stand out in this passage:

Learn to know God.
Serve him with your whole heart and a willing mind.
If you seek Him, you will find Him.
If you forsake Him, he will reject you.

Good advice for sons and daughters and moms and dads today.

RESPOND

Which of the four points made by David do you feel is most important in our world?

What might happen if today's leaders chose only one of David's four points of advice?

What might happen if *you* embraced this advice?

Dem Bones

LEARN

After finishing the book of Ezekiel, the most colorful prophet, this week we will journey into Daniel and read his entire book. Ezekiel's writings will conclude after his prophecies to foreign nations, seen in chapters 25–32. From Ezekiel 33–48, there will be a glimmer of hope with his forecast of restoration. Don't avoid tough passages. Consider reading them in a friendlier translation such as *The Message* or *God's Word*.

Daniel is familiar to Christians, and his story is matter for many sermons. Hundreds of books have been written on and around the man and his writings. The most famous Sunday school stories of a lion's den and a fiery furnace come from Daniel's experiences. Daniel was exiled to Babylon as a teenager. He was drafted into Nebuchadnezzar's service and confined to the palace. Resist the temptation to rush through Daniel's familiar story after perhaps struggling through Ezekiel. Daniel has much to say to encourage us in our world today.

READ

Day One	Ezekiel 25-29
Day Two	Ezekiel 30-32
Day Three	Ezekiel 33-35
Day Four	Ezekiel 36-39
Day Five	Ezekiel 40-48
Day Six	Daniel 1-6
Day Seven	Daniel 7-12

CONSIDER

The most famous chapter in Ezekiel was in this week's reading: chapter 37, dem bones, dem bones, dem dry bones. The most overlooked verse in the entire book is verse 3 (NLT): "'O Sovereign LORD,' I replied, "you alone know the answer to that." God had shown Ezekiel the valley of dry bones and asked him if they could live again. Ezekiel's answer is like those we use with God in various forms today: "IDK, no idea, beats me, I don't know." Ezekiel probably shrugged his shoulders and shook his head as if to say, "How should I know?"

As the headlines of today scream into our lives about the pandemic, racial unrest, political corruption, death and destruction, we ask ourselves, is there any hope? "I don't know" is the first answer that springs to mind. It seems hopeless. Impossible, dreadful, doomed. At the end of our ability. No clue how to move forward. Silence in the heavens. Right where we need to be.

When we come to the end of all human resource, God can move. It is in this place that He can shake our dry hearts, for in this place He has our undivided attention. In this place, we begin to reconnect with Him and His words. In this place, He can heal, soothe, and raise hope. I don't know why cancer invades the body, why mass murderers walk into a grocery store, why a child will be abused every ten seconds today, or why 6,435 veterans took their life last year. I don't know how to stop this. But I know who does.

RESPOND

Where do you think the bones in that valley came from?

What might dry bones represent in your life?

Recall a time when you were in a place of hopelessness. How did that situation end?

To Be Used by God

LEARN

Thessalonica and Crete are two of the few locations mentioned in the New Testament that still exist today, both in Greece. Colossae, Philemon's home, was destroyed in the twelfth century. Nevertheless, all three locations hold significance in our reading this week.

Paul wrote two letters to the Thessalonians in 51 AD. He had been run out of the city by renegade Jews who did not want Christ preached. He sent Timothy to check on the fledging church while he stayed in Corinth. Timothy's report prompted the first letter with the second following only a few months later. Timothy reported that the congregation was suffering persecution from the hostile Jews. Paul's first letter was intended to give instruction on godly living and clarify certain beliefs. His second letter was to encourage them and urge them to live self-controlled lives. In both letters he wrote extensively about the end of time on Earth.

His more personal letter to Titus was written in 65 or 66 AD. Titus and Paul had established a church on the island of Crete in between the times of Paul's imprisonments. Titus had stayed behind to disciple the church. Paul's letter was a blueprint for an orderly church written to help Titus lead the church. Paul writes about the qualifications for elders and what people in general should do to grow spiritually. He addresses responsibility to civil and governmental authority.

In an even more personal letter to Philemon in 62 AD, Paul deals with Philemon's problem with Onesimus. Onesimus was a slave in Philemon's household who had run away to Rome. He likely had been imprisoned and met Paul there. In a "six degrees of separation" type of scenario, they discover that Paul knows Onesimus's owner. This book might seem out of place in God's Word, but read on.

The readings this week are purposefully brief to encourage you to delve into the meaning behind each passage. Try reading in several translations and/or check out study notes to enhance your understanding.

READ

Day One   1 Thessalonians 1–3
Day Two   1 Thessalonians 4–5

CONSIDER

These four letters differ in theme and focus, but they all point to grace, the unmerited favor of God coupled with forgiveness. Considering the price Christ paid, we need to be sure He's getting his money's worth. We must be worthy of the call. Paul told the Ephesians this in Ephesians 4:1.

In Philemon we see an escaped servant who had stolen from his master and was imprisoned, deserving of death in that culture. Yet Paul dared to petition Philemon on his behalf. He asked Philemon not only to forgive Onesimus but to let him stay with Paul to be a help to him. This would require a master relinquishing his right to his property. Paul writes, "And I am praying that you will put into action the generosity that comes from your faith as you understand and experience all the good things we have in Christ. . . . I am confident as I write this letter that you will do what I ask and even more!" (Philemon vv. 6, 21 NLT). Paul was asking Philemon to extend grace to Onesimus, which would then demonstrate his devotion to the call of Christ.

In the book of Titus Paul gives strict instructions to servants such as Onesimus. He reminds all Christians that godly living will show others that the "grace of God has been revealed, bringing salvation to all people" (Titus 2:11 NLT). The whole book tells us how to be worthy of the call.

The words regarding the end times in the books of Thessalonians are a masterpiece of grace. We, like the people of Thessalonica, have done nothing to deserve eternal security in a place of love and joy. For some the journey will be rough, but all who endure are promised salvation. Indeed, Paul reminds us to live a life worthy of our call. *The Pulpit Commentary* explains, "The calling was, properly speaking, only the commencement of the Christian life, but as it was the first link in a chain that terminated in glory."[15] When we accept Christ into our lives, we receive a call—a call to "to do what is right, to love mercy, and to walk humbly with your God" (Micah 6:8 NLT). It is the first step to our entire life's journey from glory to glory. Our words and our actions determine the evaluation of that call.

RESPOND

Have you, like Philemon, been asked to relinquish something of great worth to you? Explain.

What could you do to walk out Titus 2?

What do you feel is your call, above and beyond Micah 6:8?

Table for Twelve

LEARN

This week is a refreshing return to complete the book of John. His writings have such a feeling of truth and love in them. John knew Jesus intimately, and these final chapters must have been difficult to write.

This week's passages from the book of John begin with the last supper and John's first memory of that night: Jesus washing the feet of his disciples. Interestingly, John does not express his feelings about this event, but he details the story of Peter's denial in verses 6–9 and 37–38 of chapter 13. He writes sadly about Jesus' predictions of his betrayal and death. John does admit to asking Jesus who the betrayer is, but he doesn't comment on his discovery, if he understood it. John 13:28–29 suggest that none of the disciples understood that Judas was the betrayer.

John records Jesus' words on this night extensively. He must have been holding on to these words with a tight grip.

In three long chapters (14–16), John explains the way to the Father, the promise of the Holy Spirit, the commandment to love, and what the world's response to the message will be. He details Jesus' prayer for himself, His prayer for his disciples, and His prayer for "for all who will ever believe in me through their message" (John 17:20 NLT). In other words, us.

John also notes the arrest, the trial, the crucifixion, the burial, and the resurrection in great detail. John understood the significance of the events after the resurrection. Jesus' actions and words after His resurrection are logged in chapters 20 and 21.

This week's readings are shorter so that your heart can "see" what John saw in these events. Read this week as though a good friend is sharing a story of his experience about a mutual friend.

READ

Day One	John 13
Day Two	John 14
Day Three	John 15-16
Day Four	John 17
Day Five	John 18-19
Day Six	John 20
Day Seven	John 21

CONSIDER

Most of this week's reading is familiar to today's Christian, especially those who have been "in the way" for a long time. Even so, the Word of God is living and active, and there is always something new to notice.

Imagine being at the last supper. It's not what most of us picture; DaVinci's portrait is beautiful, but not accurate.

In Jesus' day, the banquet table in the upper room of a home was U-shaped. The servants served from the middle. It was low to the floor with pillows for the diners to recline against. Lying on their left side with their right hand free, their feet stretched out behind them, the lowest servant could easily wash their feet.

Significantly, the seating of the guests was a deliberate act of tradition and custom. The host at this dinner, Jesus, sat in the second seat on the left. The first and third seats would be for honored guests with the others seated in order of importance. The least honored guest would be at the end of the U on the right side, yards away from the host, blocked by a servant and nearest the basin used for foot washing.

According to the scripture reading for this week, John had to be seated at Jesus' right. Peter had to be seated far enough way that he could not speak to Jesus but close enough to gesture to John. Peter had quite possibly the least important seat across the table.

The most honored and respected guest would sit at the left of the host and share the bowl with the host. At this last supper, that seat was given to . . . Judas.

I want to believe Judas elbowed his way into that seat. But because of what I know about Jesus, I believe He invited Judas to sit there. It was as if He was saying, "Here it is, Judas, one last opportunity to choose me. One last time to show you how much I love you. Take one more chance to change your mind." Then Jesus washed every disciple, even Judas's feet. More beautiful than DaVinci's painting was this portrait of forgiveness and love.

RESPOND

Where might you have sat at the last supper? Why?

Why do you think Judas sat in the most honored seat?

Which of the Gospels did you most enjoy reading? Why?

Contact the Law Offices of . . .

LEARN

This week we will make our way through the remainder of the book of Leviticus, finishing the regulations regarding feasts and festivals. The laws of Leviticus were not all restrictive. The Israelites had permission to celebrate everything! Some scholars believe these feasts were part of a prophetic calendar because they set forth the events that would accompany Christ's life on Earth. To keep the rich from accumulating too much wealth, a year of Jubilee was decreed, as we read in chapter 25. There were rewards for obedience and punishments for disobedience.

Midweek we will move on to the book of Numbers. The Hebrew Old Testament called this book "In the Desert." Translators called it "Numbers" due to the census that takes place twice and the land divisions that make up most of its content. Moses wrote the narrative in 1405 BC to explain why the Israelites did not go nonstop from Mount Sinai to the promised land. If you've read this far, you know why. Once again, in these chapters, God gives explicit instructions for the procedures and processes of life in this promised land.

READ

Day One	Leviticus 18-19
Day Two	Leviticus 20-22
Day Three	Leviticus 23-25
Day Four	Leviticus 26-27
Day Five	Numbers 1-4
Day Six	Numbers 5-7
Day Seven	Numbers 8-10

CONSIDER

The theme of Leviticus is holiness. The last nine chapters of Leviticus discuss how to relate to a holy God. They were written to the Levites, who were living in a different time and place. They worshipped in a portable tabernacle. The Levites were the mediator for the people, who could not approach God on their own. Even the Levites could only approach God with the proper sacrifices offered by explicit instruction. The entire ritual was clothed in holiness. The people of Israel were to be set apart from the rest of the world.

The first ten chapters of Numbers are preparation for entering the promised land. The census in chapter 2, the camp arrangement in chapter 2, and the unending list of offerings in chapter 7 seem to be useless information. And are, if not given a closer look.

The phrase "who were able to go to war" occurs fourteen times in Numbers chapter 1. God knew these people would have to fight for their inheritance. Throughout Exodus, He had promised to go before them and guide them. He had done so with an unnatural cloud by day and fire by night. The census and the camp diagram were further examples of God going before them.

The information in chapter 7 is the outward display of the men "who were counted" (Numbers 7:2 NIV). They showed their obedience by bringing offerings according to the previous laws they had been given. It's one of the only times Moses records the entire nation of Israel being in obedience and agreement.

In our continued reading of Numbers in a few weeks, we will read "God is not a man, so he does not lie. He is not human, so he does not change his mind. Has he ever spoken and failed to act? Has he ever promised and not carried it through?" (Numbers 23:19 NLT). The same God who numbered the men "who were able to go to war" is the God who today numbers us among those who can stand firm for Him. He has gone before us to give us victory as He promised.

RESPOND

How would you define holiness?

The Nazirite vow required outward signs of holiness (Numbers 6). What do you think are outward signs of holiness today?

What if your body of believers "numbered" those able to go into spiritual warfare; would you be counted? Why or why not?

Kings and More Kings

LEARN

The second book of Kings resumes the story of Israel and Judah's decline. The author is undisclosed, but the book was written in 560–550 BC. The author hoped that knowing the history of their divided nation would keep them from repeating the sins of their ancestors. The number of kings that came and went during these years illustrates the instability of the nations.

The stories of the prophets Elijah and Elisha are woven into the history. These are two of the most famous prophets of the Bible. Their stories are in stark contrast to the kings to whom they prophesied. Chapters 2–8 focus on Elisha's share in this history.

Remember that the writers of 1 and 2 Kings judged the performance of each king by their behavior and were clear in their conclusions. We won't be reading about too many heroes. Yet God continued to keep his promise to David throughout history despite these guys.

READ

CONSIDER

The second report card on the kings of Israel and Judah is no better than the first. The book opens with King Ahaziah sending messengers to consult Baal, an idol, about his health. Elijah intercepts them on the road and asks a poignant question from God: "Is it because there is no God in Israel?" (2 Kings 1:6 NIV). He already knew the answer. This king was Elijah's final burden, as he would soon after go to heaven in a whirlwind, leaving Elisha to deal with the rest.

We read about twenty-seven kings this week. Twenty-one of them, it was said each time, "did what was evil in the LORD's sight." None of the kings of Israel escaped this verdict. It is disturbing that the writer wrote Hoshea was less evil than most. As 2 Kings 17:2 (NIV) says, "He did evil in the eyes of the Lord, but not like the kings of Israel who preceded him." Commentators agree that while Hoshea was indeed evil, he did not personally worship false gods or compel others to do so. The lesser of two evils seemed to be accepted.

Even the six kings of Judah who were not called evil tolerated idolatry, choosing not to destroy the temples of idols. The book is full of conspiracies and murders. It's no wonder God allowed these people to be exiled into captivity.

Yet God still had a covenant with David. A covenant differs from a contract in that a covenant is not dependent on what the other party does or does not do. God's promise that David's family would always have a king was not dependent on the behavior of the people of Israel. Chapter 11 of our reading illustrates this. Athaliah, by mass murder, makes herself queen, the only ruler not of Davidic descent ever to reign on Judah's throne. It appeared that David's line had been broken and God's promise had failed. There was no human way to restore David's descendants to the throne. Athaliah doesn't know for six years that her grandson survived her murders and has been hidden by the high priest. The high priest makes the six-year-old king, and Athaliah meets the fate she meted out to others. Judah's throne is once again in the hands of David's descendants.

God always honors His promises. The history readings of the Old Testament prove it time and time again. Why would the Israelites doubt the promise of a coming Messiah? Why would we doubt His return?

RESPOND

Which of these kings has intrigued you? Why?

Were you familiar with the story of Elisha? What stood out in this week's reading about him?

What is the purpose of retelling the same stories in different books of the Bible?

Deeper, Deeper

LEARN

This week's reading will take us deeper into the records of some of the kings we read about last week. Second Chronicles 21 will revisit the reigns of Jehoram and Ahaziah and a retelling of the wicked Athaliah. These chapters will give us a deeper dive into little Joash's reign and his downfall after the death of Jehoiada, the high priest who had saved his life. Among the kings we will read more about are Hezekiah, Jehoshaphat, and Ahaz. Observe Hezekiah's actions in 2 Chronicles 30 as he strives to return to the God of their fathers.

Psalms are always uplifting when coupled with not-so-pleasant history. Suzanna Wesley, mother of John and Charles Wesley, told her boys, "Fall in love with Psalm 119 and you will love the whole Bible." As we observe Hezekiah's Passover celebration in 2 Chronicles 30, we also read Psalms 113–118 as the songs of Passover. Consider the parallels between the Psalms and the actions of the evil kings.

READ

Day One	Psalm 107–112
Day Two	2 Chronicles 21–24
Day Three	2 Chronicles 25–28
Day Four	2 Chronicles 29–31
Day Five	Psalms 113–118
Day Six	2 Chronicles 32–36
Day Seven	Psalms 119–121

CONSIDER

The King Hezekiah of Sunday school had one story. He's the main character in the miracle of the backward sun (see Isaiah 38). He got very sick, was about to die, but he prayed to live. God heard and gave him fifteen more years of life. God sealed the deal by moving the sun's shadow ten steps backward on a sundial. Never happened before, never happened since. Without the reading of 2 Kings and 2 Chronicles, one would never know how important Hezekiah was to Israel's history.

The son of King Ahaz, among the most wicked kings of Judah, Hezekiah somehow grew into integrity and honesty. Maybe it was his mom, Abijah, daughter of Zechariah.

Second Chronicles 29:2 (NIV) says that Hezekiah "did what was right in the eyes of the LORD." A nice departure from all the other kings, including his father, doing "evil in the eyes of the Lord." In the first month of Hezekiah's reign, he opened and repaired the temple. He brought the Levites back and ordered them to consecrate themselves. After they had purified themselves and the temple, he reinstated burnt offerings. The people returned to the Law of Moses in every way. Throughout Judah, Hezekiah did what was good, right, and faithful.

The Passover had not been celebrated in large numbers for many years. Hezekiah called the people to Jerusalem to reinstate it. Psalms 113–118 are called the "Passover Psalms," and they are read to this day in Jewish homes on Passover. No doubt, they were read at this Passover also.

Hezekiah is a standard of free will. Despite his wicked father as well as the years and years of evil among the kings of Judah, he made different choices. He did what he could and left the rest to God. He could have been hampered by his past, but he was not. Hezekiah is a bright spot in the history of Judah's kings. We would do well to be defined by our future, not our past.

RESPOND

Did you grow up in a Christian home? How did that impact your walk with the Lord?

Did anything in the Psalms parallel the stories of any of the other kings?

Why would Suzanna Wesley have put so much significance on Psalm 119?

A King's Heart

LEARN

Tradition holds that Ezra, a priest and a scribe, collected the Old Testament books as a unit. He quite possibly contributed to the history written in all the Old Testament books. Undoubtedly, Ezra wrote the book named after him, probably around 450–420 BC. Ezra continues the tale of the Jews after their exile to Babylon. His writings confirm the prophecies of Jeremiah and Isaiah that God would restore the people (see Jeremiah 29:10–14 and Isaiah 44:24–28). Particularly interesting is the account of God's power among the Persian kings. Ezra's account involves three Persian kings and five well-respected spiritual leaders. These were the men who made life-and-death decisions about the Jewish people. It is important to note that between chapters 6 and 7 of Ezra is a forty-year gap. During that gap the story of Queen Esther emerges. Look for some familiar names in this book, such as Haggai, Zechariah, and Mordecai.

Ezra's historical account includes references to the prophecies of Zechariah as well. Zechariah prophesied alongside Haggai in post-exile Judah, the period written about in the book of Ezra. Zechariah's first eight chapters are prophetic to Ezra's time period, but the last six were likely written by an aging Zechariah. Zechariah's writings as compared to Ezra's narrative are puzzling, as Nick Page points out in his book *The MAP: Making the Bible Meaningful, Accessible, Practical*: "Many experts . . . spent long hours studying the text [Zechariah] only to be forced to concede that they have no idea what the prophet is going on about."[16] Despite this, all agree that one thing he is saying is that a king will reign in Jerusalem again someday. Who knew these two little books could be so exciting?

READ

Day One	Ezra 1–6
Day Two	Ezra 7–8
Day Three	Zechariah 1–5
Day Four	Zechariah 6–8
Day Five	Ezra 9–10
Day Six	Zechariah 9–11
Day Seven	Zechariah 12–14

CONSIDER

The first exiles returning to Jerusalem were living under the reign of Cyrus. Cyrus was to the Babylonians what Moses was for the Israelites. He was brave and daring as well as tolerant and benevolent. Perhaps the latter trait played into his decision to free the Israelites. However, as Ezra 1:1 (NLT) says, God "stirred the heart of Cyrus to put this proclamation in writing." The proclamation said anyone who wanted to return to Jerusalem to build the temple of their God could do so.

But there were enemies of Judah who tried to stop the rebuilding of the temple. They wrote a letter to King Darius in 516 BC imploring his help. Darius was a brilliant administrator and well-known for his outlandish building projects. He imposed his rule by force, so his favorable response to the Israelites, in Ezra 6:3–5, seems a bit out of character.

Ezra's book fades out for the next sixty years when Xerxes is king, grabs a Jewish girl for queen, and if you don't know that story, we'll read it later. At any rate, the Jews get to keep building their temple and don't get annihilated during this time. Xerxes is eventually murdered by his own captain of the guard, who then makes Artaxerxes king.

During this action, Zechariah is prophesying up a storm with eight visions in one night, chapters 1–6. These visions conjure up memories of what the people have gone through and why. Conversely, they also give insight to restoration, removal of sin, and the coming happy ending. Five hundred years before Jesus would come as a baby in a manger, this colorful prophet speaks of thirty pieces of silver, looking at one pierced by the Jews, and a shepherd whose sheep will scatter. All of which later happened, of course.

Ezra's writings return sixty years later in chapter 7. Ezra returns to Jerusalem as the leader of the former exiles. King Artaxerxes sends him on his way with a letter and luggage full of silver and gold from the "province of Babylon" (Ezra 7:16).

Three Persian kings, none of whom acknowledged the God of Israel, gave their blessing to the very people they had kidnapped and carried away into exile. They freed them to build a temple to a God they regarded no more powerful than their own idols. One generous king paid them for their trouble. If God can move the hearts of kings, He can move the hearts of our politicians today.

RESPOND

How would you compare the happenings of Ezra's days to
those in America today?

Do you believe our current government is favorable toward
God's people? Why or why not?

In Ezra 6, Darius found a stored scroll that clarified what his
position should be. Are there any documents that should be
found and reread by our government?

Majoring in the Minors

LEARN

The five books of prophecy this week are minor, not because they are less important but because they are smaller in size. The word *minor* doesn't negate any of their words or minimize their message. To the contrary, many of the prophecies contained here point directly to the Messiah and provide hope for the future.

These prophets spoke to the nation of Judah before the exile between 835 and 606 BC. All warned the nation of Israel about upcoming judgment if they didn't repent. All knew the history of this idolatrous and sinful nation. They each came from different backgrounds.

Joel had extensive knowledge of the priesthood, indicating he might have lived in Jerusalem. Micah was a country preacher from a small agricultural area. Nahum's name meant "comfort";

his book was everything but. He came from Elkosh, a town so small no one is sure where it was located. Habakkuk calls himself a prophet, and some clues indicate he may have been a Levite musician in Jerusalem. Zephaniah was the great-great-grandson of King Hezekiah, giving him access to the palace and capitol in Jerusalem.

This mixed bag of writers carried a message from God with a consistent theme: *"Repent or else. And even if you don't, I, God, will never give up on you or stop loving you."* Their harsh words of judgment are brutal and even frightening. Zephaniah's first chapter reads like a horror film. The locust plague in Joel rivals some of the stories from Exodus. Nahum has only bad news for Nineveh. Don't miss the glimmers of hope that weave in and out of this week's reading.

READ

Day One	Joel 1-3
Day Two	Micah 1-2
Day Three	Micah 3-4
Day Four	Micah 5-7
Day Five	Nahum 1-3
Day Six	Habakkuk 1-3
Day Seven	Zephaniah 1-3

CONSIDER

Throughout these five books of prophecy are four main points: repentance, warning of judgment, promise of deliverance, and hope for a future.

All five authors have harsh vocabulary for those who refuse to hear God's word. Joel calls it "a day of darkness and gloom" (Joel 2:2 NIV). Micah clarifies that this disaster has come from the Lord (Micah 1:12). The terrifying words from God "I am against you" are repeated twice in Nahum (Nahum 2:13; 3:5 NIV). Habakkuk enumerates the five "woes" because of the sin of the nation (Habakkuk 2). Zechariah says there will be a day of wrath, distress, and anguish (Zechariah 1:15).

Thinking back on the history of this nation, do they deserve any less? From the day they left Egypt, they have been nothing but disobedient, idolatrous, and sinful. This is righteous judgment, judgment that was threatened time and time again. Yet the power of yet. Yet says that there is still hope, things can still turn around, even in the face of sin, rebellion, failures. Even still, yet the Lord offers to be gracious and give mercy.

Each of these prophets ends his message with hope and deliverance for the repentant. The God of Israel never gives up on this wicked nation. He gives them chance after chance to repent. He is always making a way out. We, too, can trust that this same God will not give up on us. If we confess our sins, repent, and stop doing wrong, we will hear Him say, "Watch—and be utterly amazed" (Habakkuk 1:5 NIV).

RESPOND

How does America compare with the Israel of the Old Testament?

Which of these prophets do you find most relevant today?

What did that prophet say that stood out to you?

Keeping the Post Office in Business

LEARN

More letters with new authors. In the book of Acts we learned of Paul and Timothy's relationship. Paul assigned Timothy to minister in Ephesus with his blessing. The two letters sent to Timothy are pastoral, as they instructed Timothy in guiding a church. Second Timothy was the last letter Paul wrote before being martyred.

James's and Jude's letters were to undisclosed "believers." These two brothers of Jesus had become Christians following Jesus' resurrection. James was believed to be the leader of the church at Jerusalem and is mentioned many times in the book of Acts. His letter has a distinctive Jewish slant. It is likely that Jude's letter was also written to Jewish Christians, as he references Moses, Cain, Balaam, Enoch, and Korah from the Old

Testament. The implication is that his readers would likely have been familiar with these names.

These letters speak to us about godliness, ten times in the letters to Timothy. They will also dare us to "contend for the faith" (Jude v. 3 NIV). Be challenged as you read.

READ

Day One	1 Timothy 1-3
Day Two	1 Timothy 4-6
Day Three	2 Timothy 1-2
Day Four	2 Timothy 3-4
Day Five	James 1-2
Day Six	James 3-4
Day Seven	Jude

CONSIDER

Two words stand out in this week's reading: *contend* and *entrusted*. *Contend* means "to uphold." The early Christians were given the message of Christ and tasked with taking it into the world. They were "entrusted" with this monumental responsibility. According to Dictionary.com, the word *entrusted* means "to invest something to someone with trust and responsibility." The Greek word is "transmitted." Another translation uses the word *deposited*. The message of Christ has been deposited into the hearts, souls, and minds of those who listen. The message of Christ is transmitted to all who choose to hear. The word *entrusted* appears in seventeen verses in the Bible. Six of those times are in the letters to Timothy. One is by Jude. James does not use the word but gives several examples of the gospel being entrusted to the people.

James's book is described as "intensely practical."[17] Some scholars don't like the book because there is not enough mention of Jesus and faith. James wasn't writing that book; he was writing a handbook of useful tips for living. They included several warnings for the good of the people. Chapter 3 begins by instructing teachers to be wary of their calling and goes right into the reason for this: the mouth. If people are listening to you, you have a greater responsibility to control what you say. He reminds us repeatedly that true wisdom comes from God. If you have been assigned, or entrusted, with wisdom or the call of teaching, "prove it by living an honorable life, doing good works with the humility that comes from wisdom" (James 3:13 NLT).

Jude says that we have been "entrusted" with faith. The Greek word for *faith* in this verse is "belief, confidence." We have been given the responsibility to fight for these beliefs, and the reward is confidence in that belief.

The letters to Timothy continue to instruct those who have been entrusted with the task of spreading the message of Christ. In 2 Timothy, Paul gives Timothy permission to delegate the message to others—with one stipulation: entrust not just those who believe. They must also be loyal, trustworthy, and courageous enough never to betray the message.

All but one use of the word *entrusted* refers to the message bearer keeping the message safe, true, and secure. In 2 Timothy 1:12, Paul uses the word about his own soul. He has entrusted his eternal self to Jesus, and he is confident in Jesus' ability to keep him through eternity.

An old hymn by Daniel W. Whittle declares, "But I know whom I have believed in and am persuaded that He is able to keep that which I've committed unto Him against that day." What is entrusted to Him is safe; may the same be said about what He entrusts to us.

RESPOND

What is something you feel God has entrusted to you? What is something you have entrusted to Him?

How do you consistently put God first in your life?

What did you think about the book of James, yay or nay? Why?

From Wimp to Warrior

LEARN

Luke's second book begins where his Gospel ends, with the ascension of Jesus into heaven. The book of Acts, written in 63 AD, begins by saying, "In my former book," alluding to the book of Luke (Acts 1:1 NIV). Both of Luke's books are written to "Theophilus," meaning "student," which indicates the book was dedicated to all students—i.e., us. The chapters we will read this week are the birth and early history of the Christian church, featuring both Paul's and Peter's ministries. Before Luke is finished, he will take us to thirty-two countries, fifty-four cities, and nine islands, and we will meet ninety-five people by name. The book is biographical, geographical, ethnical, and doctrinal. Pentecost is a central part of this text before the story of Paul takes over. Paul overshadows so much of this book, it's easy to miss the importance of Peter's ministry, especially since he isn't mentioned again after chapter 12.

This week's readings will contain the most famous verses of Acts, those that describe the baptism of the Holy Spirit. Throughout the book we will read about that power. It changed a traitor and liar, a murderer, and many others with stories much like ours. It is the story of a group of ordinary men carrying out the mission of the Son of the Living God because of a supernatural power. Do not read it as simply history; read it as a handbook for your life.

READ

Day One	Acts 1-2
Day Two	Acts 3-4
Day Three	Acts 5-6
Day Four	Acts 7
Day Five	Acts 8-9
Day Six	Acts 10
Day Seven	Acts 11-12

CONSIDER

Within the genre context, Acts falls in line with the Gospels, although it is clearly a history of the early church. That said, the Gospels represent the proclamation of Christ, and Acts certainly fits that definition. The contents of Acts mirror the difficulties and victories of today's church, making it one of the most relevant biblical books. The book begins with Pentecost taking place about ten days after Jesus ascended to heaven, an event that transformed a band of frightened, timid, heartbroken men and women who were firsthand witnesses of Jesus' life on Earth. Not the least of which was a man named Simon Peter.

Acts 4–6 are the record of this traitor's dramatic change. After a mighty wind sweeps into the room where he and his friends are "waiting," tongues of fire sit on their heads and don't burn their hair, and they speak in many different languages. Peter then stands up and preaches the greatest sermon of all time. He lends credence to his message by quoting the Jewish prophet Joel. Three thousand Jews believe the message and are converted. The birth of the church. Peter and John are brought to the Sanhedrin, the Jewish ruling counsel, to explain this "power" they've been preaching about. Some familiar names noted here include Annas and Caiaphas, who might be remembered from other Gospel writings. Peter and John have been emboldened by this baptism of the Holy Spirit: "We cannot help speaking about what we have seen and heard" (Acts 4:19 NIV); "We must obey God rather than men" (Acts 5:29 ESV). The Scripture goes on to say, "They took note that these men had been with Jesus" (Acts 4:13 NIV). The members of the Jewish ruling council understood these were the disciples of Jesus. This is not only a reference to their physical proximity to Jesus but also to the courage and freedom with which they spoke. Ellicott comments that they displayed complete "confidence in approaching God."[18]

Luke continues, saying that not everything went well. The unbelieving Jews persecute and even kill many of those spreading the message. Peter, on assignment from God, opens salvation to the Gentiles, which becomes a sticky wicket (but aren't you grateful he did?). Suddenly from out of nowhere, Peter's complete opposite, Saul, comes into the story. This will get interesting.

RESPOND

Explore your beliefs about Pentecost, as described in Acts 2.

Who are you in this story of the early church? Why?

Why do you suppose Luke doesn't mention Peter again after chapter 12?

You Protest Too Much, All the time

LEARN

The book of Numbers could be called the book of grumbling. As the Israelites made their way to the land of milk and honey promised to their forefathers, they couldn't keep it together. They were discontented and complaining. They became more and more rebellious, according to the passages in our reading this week. Not surprisingly, rebellion led to disobedience, which translated into sin.

The patience of God wore out with these people, as seen in chapter 13. We will read about the twelve spies who went to Canaan to stake out the land. This was the land God had promised them, in fact, continued to promise them in spite of their idolatry. They were on the brink of the guarantee. Ten of twelve said, it's too hard, we can't do it; it will never work; it's not going to happen. In essence, they were saying, God is wrong, we can't have the land. He lied. The unbelief of ten men were unmoved by God's faithfulness thus far. The unbelief of ten men kept an entire generation from their destiny. The remaining chapters of Numbers will not be boring. Look for flickers of God's grace among these stubborn people.

READ

Day One	Numbers 11–14
Day Two	Numbers 15–19
Day Three	Numbers 20–25
Day Four	Numbers 26
Day Five	Numbers 27–30
Day Six	Numbers 31–33
Day Seven	Numbers 34–36

CONSIDER

It's tempting to judge these wanderers harshly. For years they had been enslaved in Egypt; they got out with wealth and goods. They had a promise from God about a land where they would have plenty of everything and life would be easy. They wandered in a desert for forty years, and their shoes never wore out. They had plenty to eat, although they complained about the menu. Standing at the edge of this promised land, just a few steps farther, and they again disobeyed. They failed to believe

God's words and idolized their life in Egypt. God had more patience than any of us would. They were told they would not enter this land, so as usual they repented for a minute. Anyone over twenty years old would die before the nation received their inheritance. Bible teacher Jabe Nicholson did the math: eighty-eight funerals a day while the generation perished.

In chapter 14 God asked Moses, "How long will these people treat me with contempt? Will they never believe me, even after all the miraculous signs I have done among them?" (Numbers 14:11 NLT). We wonder the same thing as we read.

Still, in the midst of discontent, rebellion, disobedience, idolatry, and complaining, the Creator of this mess of a people continued to give grace. Complaints about the manna brought quail. Rivalry among the tribes caused God to desire to destroy them, but instead he caused Aaron's staff to bud as a warning, not a sentence. Lack of water was met with a gushing rock. Hundreds died from snake bite, yet many survived by looking at a bronze snake on a pole. Balaam was unable to curse Israel no matter how hard he tried. During the entire journey, God's people were led by a cloud by day and fire by night. Only God's grace preserved this nation.

We live in a world of discontent, rebellion, disobedience, idolatry, and complaining. Someone once said, we should not wonder at the evil of our world; we should wonder that there is not more. Except for grace.

RESPOND

Where have you seen God's patience with you?

Is there something in your past you look back to and long for? Is it time to let it go?

How have you seen grace manifest even in the midst of your rebellion or discontent?

The Minor Leagues

LEARN

Obadiah was a prophet who prophesied in 840 BC during the exile of the Jewish people. He spoke specifically to the Edomites, who were rejoicing over Israel's troubles. Israel is God's chosen and beloved nation, so it will never do to be against them.

Haggai prophesied in 520 BC to the Jewish people returning to Jerusalem. Ezra mentions him several times as one who was encouraging the rebuilding of the temple. The book of Haggai only contains four messages within two chapters, which Haggai would have delivered within four months. Each chapter makes it clear that it is a "word" from the Lord. In 430–420 BC, the Jewish exiles were being allowed to return to their homeland. Nehemiah, an exiled Jew, was working as a cupbearer to King Artaxerxes. Ezra was already rebuilding the temple, and it was in Nehemiah's heart to rebuild the walls of the city. Once again God turns the heart of a Persian king, who allows Nehemiah to go with his blessing and materials to do the building. Yet another prophet prophesying during this time was Malachi. He was a priestly prophet who spoke to the people likely after the temple had been built and during the wall project.

Again, these "minor" prophets are not called thus because of their insignificance. Their writings were as inspired as any other scriptures. Read "the Word of the Lord" given to these specific prophets for a specific time yet which is still meaningful today.

READ

Day One	Obadiah
Day Two	Haggai
Day Three	Malachi
Day Four	Nehemiah 1-2
Day Five	Nehemiah 3-7
Day Six	Nehemiah 8-10
Day Seven	Nehemiah 11-13

CONSIDER

Most of the books of the Old Testament can be classified as prophecy. The wonder is that fifteen different authors foretold the future of the Jewish and Gentile nation over a period of four thousand years. The next largest group of books in the Bible is history. Paul called every word of these writings inspired, useful, and corrective. Many translations call the Bible "God-breathed." Even as the reader stumbles through minor prophets and repetitive history, it is well to remember that every word had a purpose.

Obadiah's twenty-one verses may seem insignificant in the big picture, but they reveal that God doesn't like it when you rejoice in another's troubles, especially His people in trouble.

Haggai seems to pressure the Jews to rebuild the temple. And he does. The underlying issue is that the people had misplaced priorities. They were fitting God into their agenda instead of allowing Him to set the agenda.

Malachi spoke to a people who had become skeptical in their beliefs. All those prophecies, sure, many of them had come true, but now, but the most important one, the coming Messiah, well . . .

The historical part of this week's reading, the book of Nehemiah, is the story of rebuilding the wall around Jerusalem. It is also the fulfillment of prophecy spoken by Daniel. Today it reminds us to stand obedient to the Word of God despite ridicule, insult, conspiracy, blackmail, or compromise.

We live today in a world of misplaced priorities, hatred among races, and prophecies unfulfilled. Life makes us skeptical about the things we've heard and seen. Proclaiming Christ brings insult, and we are pressed to compromise in the name of tolerance. We, too, have been waiting for the return of that Messiah.

God is still speaking through the prophets of old, to a world vastly different today, yet He remains relevant.

RESPOND

Nehemiah's mandate was rebuild, restore, repent, and return. In your life, what needs to be rebuilt? Restored? Forgiven? Returned to?

What needs to be done for you to return to God and His plans for you?

Which of the three prophecies that you read this week impacted you the most? Why?

Multipurpose Songs

LEARN

Wrapping up the book of Psalms will be a bittersweet experience. So much emotion is evident in every word. We finish this book of praise and wonder with a renewed love for the Word of God.[19]

The first twelve Psalms read this week are called "songs of ascents." David wrote four of them, Solomon wrote one, and the others are anonymous. Jerusalem was situated on a high hill; when the people traveled there for festivals, these are the songs they sang on their way. They may not have been written for this purpose, but tradition says they have been grouped together for the purpose of singing while traveling. Each song of ascent has a specific theme of encouragement for our worship today as well. Read to identify these themes throughout the week.

READ

Day One	Psalms 122-126
Day Two	Psalms 127-131
Day Three	Psalms 132-135
Day Four	Psalms 136-139
Day Five	Psalms 140-144
Day Six	Psalms 145-147
Day Seven	Psalms 148-150

CONSIDER

Amazon boasts over ten thousand results for books on praying Scripture. Authors such as Ann Voskamp, Jodie Berndt, Kenneth Boa, and Beth Moore have penned missives on the subject. A quick Google search will yield thousands of blog posts. Among the reasons for praying Scripture: praying God's own words makes us confident that we are praying in the will of God and assures us that we are praying truth. Evan Howard, in his book *Praying the Scriptures: A Field Guide for Your Spiritual Journey*, writes, "To pray the Scriptures is to order one's time of prayer around a particular text in the Bible."[20] How powerful that becomes when choosing a scripture pertinent to a situation in your own life.

The Psalms are the perfect place to learn to pray Scripture. For example, Psalm 123:3–4 (NLT) says, " Have mercy on us,

LORD, have mercy, for we have had our fill of contempt. We have had more than our fill of the scoffing of the proud and the contempt of the arrogant." I know I have.

During a sleepless night, pray the words of Psalm 127:2 (NIV): "Grant sleep to me, for I know I am loved."

In times of trouble, pray Psalm 130:2 (NIV): "Lord, hear my cry, let your ears be attentive to my cry for mercy."

Teach your kids Psalm 133:1 (NLT): " How wonderful and pleasant it is when brothers live in harmony."

When facing death, read Psalm 139:13–16.

When you have sinned, go to Psalm 139:23–24.

When alone, refer to Psalm 145:18.

Previously, we read that the book of Psalms is a divine hymnal; there is a song for every person in every circumstance.

The final Psalm, 150, is a song of ultimate praise—an answer to the questions of where, why, and how the Lord should be praised.

Where? Everywhere. Why? He is great and powerful. How? Music, dancing, in every way imaginable. "Let everything that has breathe praise the LORD" (Psalm 150:6 NIV).

Praise is linked with worship. The church has praise and worship every service. It's easy to see them as synonymous, but they are not. Praise is universal; it can be lavished on anyone whom we deem deserving. In the church, praise is a joyful utterance about all God has done for us. It includes thanksgiving. Worship, on the other hand, is for God alone. Worship is surrendering ourselves and all within us to God. Worship is an attitude of the heart. These songs of ascent should be part of our praise and worship. Because we, too, are on ascent—climbing our life's path to a home with Jesus.

In case you need the themes for the ascent songs, here they are:

Psalm 122 (prayers for Jerusalem)

Psalm 123 (waiting for mercy)

Psalm 124 (help from the Lord)

Psalm 125 (God's blessing)

Psalm 126 (the Lord does great things)

Psalm 127 (bless our efforts)

Psalm 128 (joy)

Psalm 129 (cries for help)

Psalm 130 (repentance)

Psalm 131 (surrender)

Psalm 132 (God's plans)

Psalm 133 (fellowship and unity

Psalm 134 (praise to God in His temple)

RESPOND

How are praise and worship different in your mind?

Have you ever prayed Scripture? What happened?

Which Psalm is your song today? Why?

Final Wise Words

LEARN

This week we will finish the Proverbs and read Solomon's dirge, the book of Ecclesiastes. In these final chapters, Solomon will continue his insight regarding the "simple." *Ellicott's Commentary* defines *simple* as those "who are open" to teaching. He says that Solomon's wisdom was based on sound reasoning. King Hezekiah's men collected the writings in Proverbs 25–29, but they are still credited to Solomon. Chapter 31, the most famous of the Proverbs, is attributed to King Lemuel. The chapter opening states that the written teachings were taught to him by his mother.

There are several theories on who this Lemuel might have been. Some believe Lemuel was a nickname Bathsheba gave to her son, Solomon. If so, chapter 31 was written in her honor and verses 10–32 describe her. Some believe King Hezekiah wrote this chapter. His mother, Abijah, was a godly woman who trained her son well despite her wicked husband. Others believe Lemuel and his mother were fictional characters developed for the sake of being Solomon's example. Regardless, the wisdom contained therein remains. Heed the advice of Proverbs 31:22:17 (NLT): "Listen to the words of the wise; apply your heart to my instruction."

Ecclesiastes, with our next set of readings for this week, was written in 935 BC toward the end of King Solomon's reign. From earlier readings, we know Solomon was the richest, wisest, and most popular king of Judah's history. Near the end of his reign and life, his many pagan wives influenced him, causing him to turn away from God. This would certainly point to the dark tone and negativity of the book. Scholars believe that this book represents excerpts from Solomon's journal. The book does not read as a story with beginning, middle, and end. The word *vanity* appears thirty-eight times in this week's reading. *Vanity* here meaning "futility, emptiness, uselessness." Landon MacDonald, a graduate of Moody college and current pastor in Phoenix, describes Ecclesiastes as vanity explained, explored, expanded, and exonerated.[21] An introspective reading will reveal that life is meaningless without God.

READ

| Day One | Proverbs 25–27 |
| Day Two | Proverbs 28–29 |

CONSIDER

King Solomon reminds us of people within our society. He was an influencer, wealthy, well-known. He was financially secure and politically savvy. Nothing (not even seven hundred women) was beyond his control. He could and did follow his every desire. Yet as he wrote, "Meaningless! Meaningless! . . . Everything is meaningless" (Ecclesiastes 1:2 NIV). These words written over two thousand years ago ring true today. It is easy, for example, to find a long list of the rich and famous who have committed suicide. Hollywood icon Marilyn Monroe left behind a note that began, "I am still lost." Freddie Prinz's note said, "There is no hope left."

Our reading of God's Word has been depressing, gory, mind-boggling, and sad, but it has never been without hope for redemption. Solomon's Ecclesiastes is no different. In the last three chapters, he reluctantly resigns himself to death, as we all must. Within these words of Ecclesiastes, he has explored the alternatives for happiness, faced the meaninglessness of them, and returned to the only truth there is: somehow God will make all of this meaningful someday. Keep on keeping on. In verse 13 of the final chapter, we read, "Everything you were taught can be put into a few words: Respect and obey God! This is what life is all about" (Ecclesiastes 12:13 CEV). Indeed, this is what a life that pleases God is all about.

RESPOND

What are your true feelings about that "Proverbs 31 woman" people always talk about?

Do you agree with Solomon that "everything is meaningless"? Why or why not?

What is the one thing you think would change your life right now? What if you obtained it?

Fish, Cheatin' Wives, and Ordinary People

LEARN

We return to the last of the prophecies this week, ending with three more minor prophets: Hosea, Amos, and Jonah. Two of the three have become famous over the years for their amazing stories.

Jonah and the whale. The story has rivaled the popular fairy tales, been told in multiple formats, and been content for children's lessons throughout history. In his story recorded in 760 BC Jonah was transparent to the northern kingdom of Israel. He wrote of his failures as well as his victories.

Hosea, the long-suffering husband of a prostitute. No other writer lived his message like Hosea. God used him as a visual example of His own love shown to a nation who constantly were unfaithful. He also wrote to the northern kingdom; his book was written in 715–710 BC. God used Hosea to personify the merciful, forgiving love God bestows on the worst of the worst. His story, like Jonah's, has been told and retold through the years.

Amos who? Amos was a common shepherd from a little village twelve miles out of Jerusalem. Amos was the epitome of "ordinary." Although he lived in Judah, he went north to preach the message, repent or perish.

The readings this week are short, and we are nearing the end of our goal. Slow down, look past the familiar, and find what the Lord would say to you.

READ

Day One	Jonah 1-4
Day Two	Hosea 1-5
Day Three	Hosea 6-10
Day Four	Hosea 11-14
Day Five	Amos 1-2
Day Six	Amos 3-6
Day Seven	Amos 7-9

CONSIDER

It is surprising how many lessons these three little-known prophets taught. All the minor prophets address social justice, the need for repentance, warnings of judgment, and the promise of a future with the coming Messiah. These three are no different.

For these prophets, disobedience was linked with idolatry. That seems to be a recurring issue in the nation of Israel, indeed the world. Jonah refused to go where God sent him. Gomer, Hosea's wayward wife, continually chose the world over her husband no matter what he did. Amos's audience was corrupt on every level.

These prophets mentioned the cost of disobedience. In the first verses of Jonah, he writes that he "bought a ticket" (Jonah 1:3 NLT). Jonah's disobedient behavior didn't only cost him three days in an underwater bed with no breakfast; he actually paid good money to avoid God's will. Additionally, his disobedience cost others peace of mind on a cruise. Disobedience always has a price.

Gomer, Hosea's wife, representing the nation of Israel, was the queen of disobedience. She was separated from her children; is there a worse fate for a mother? This is the woman of whom Hosea said will "reap the whirlwind" (Hosea 8:7 NIV). No one wants to be in a tornado, I know.

Amos promised the people that their disobedience would cost them their freedom and property.

Still, God always, always revealed a way out. Songwriters and preachers say you can't go too far from God; you can't do anything too bad that He'll give up on you. The Old Testament is a testimony of this. Think back at everything Israel did after the move out of Egypt. Here, thousands of years later, God is still in a forgiving mood. True repentance was always met with forgiveness. There was always a way to start over. Still is.

RESPOND

What has been the cost of your disobedience?

How have you experienced the mercy of God?

Do you see yourself as "ordinary"? What can God do with that?

A Never-Ending Story

LEARN

Our final reading through the book of Acts will focus entirely on Paul following his conversion. It is the record of his three famous missionary journeys through Asia and modern-day Europe.

Acts 13–15 report journey number one taking place about fifteen years after Jesus' resurrection. Barnabus, aka Joseph, a Levite from, Cyprus was Paul's traveling companion. Barnabus was introduced earlier in Acts 4:36. He sold some land and gave all the proceeds to the work of Christ. We will learn this isn't the only reason the disciples nicknamed him Barnabus, which means son of encouragement. This trip lasted about eighteen months. Paul established his pattern of presenting himself in the town synagogue and speaking to the Jewish leaders first. As they invariably opposed his message, he went to the Gentiles. Signs and wonders accompanied his ministry as God intended. It was also accompanied by trial and hardship. At one stop, Paul was stoned and left for dead. He and Barnabus were abandoned by a young man, John Mark. Their disagreement over him led to a separation of the two missionaries.

Paul's second journey is recorded in chapters 16–18. Due to his separation from Barnabus, he chose a new companion, Silas, and invited a young man from Lystra, Timothy, for this trip. Timothy traveled with them for about three and a half months. Beatings, prison, and persecution would follow them on this road, yet the planting of many churches would bring great joy.

Finally, Paul will make his last journey in chapters 19–21. There is no record of who accompanied Paul on this journey; however, he rarely traveled alone. Scholars believe Silas and Timothy probably were with him on this trip also. It lasted three months and was much the same as the previous tours.

The book of Acts will fade away with Paul arrested in Jerusalem, transported to Caesarea for trial, and after a harrowing cruise, imprisoned in Rome. Jhumpa Lahiri, an American author, said, "That's the thing about books. They let you travel without moving your feet." Have a nice trip this week.

READ

Day One	Acts 13
Day Two	Acts 14–15
Day Three	Acts 16–18

Day Four	Acts 19–21
Day Five	Acts 22–23
Day Six	Acts 24–26
Day Seven	Acts 27–28

CONSIDER

In the genre realm, this is the final book of Gospel writing. The remaining books of the Bible are letters to churches and individuals who lived during the early years of Christianity. There is no more history recorded, no more poetry, and only one prophecy. Scholars believe Paul continued to live in Rome, under house arrest for the next two years. He received visitors, proclaimed the kingdom of God and continued teaching about Jesus. He wrote his last letter, 2 Timothy, during this time and was never heard from again. Jewish tradition believes he was executed in 67 AD.

Every commentator, scholar, and teacher comments on Luke's ending of this book. It is not textbook. It ends abruptly, some say with no ending at all. Given Luke's writing ability and the detail in his previous writings, this is puzzling. Except . . . the book of Acts is the story of the church of Jesus Christ. Down through the ages, the church has gone underground, and the message has been diluted to be socially attractive. The church has been misrepresented, exalted, and scorned. Skepticism has not stopped this message. A message that started in an upper room carried by men and women who couldn't help but tell what they had seen and heard, no matter the cost. Because they had been with Jesus.

Luke did not give the book of Acts an ending because it has not ended yet.

RESPOND

How do you respond to the idea that the book has not ended?

What if you had accompanied Paul on one of his journeys—which one would you have chosen and why?

What other hardships might Paul and his companions have encountered while traveling in this time period?

No More Mail

LEARN

Peter makes his final appearance in the Bible this week with two letters written to anybody who will listen. Peter's ministry was characterized by that audience. Peter talked to anyone who would listen. He writes these letters in 62 and 66 AD, the latter being near the end of his life. There is some controversy today about the authorship of these two letters. Many believe they are not Peter's writings due to the inconsistencies in style and perfecting of the Greek. The second letter is much less polished and unrefined, giving some the idea that two different writers penned the letters. Peter, however, identifies himself as the writer of both. In 1 Peter 5:12, he states that Silas helped him. The second letter makes no such claim, implying that Peter wrote it himself without the benefit of an editor. This is yet another example of the enemy's mission to somehow discredit the Word of God. Whoever wrote 2 Peter, it was an inspired message and has stood the test of time.

On the other hand, some say the book of Hebrews was written by an unknown author to an unknown audience. Its content points to issues important to Jewish Christians, probably in Rome. Christianity wasn't popular. The former Jews had given up their beautiful temples, their showy festivals, their standing with the government (oppressive as it was) for house churches filled with slaves, widows, orphans, and ex-pagans. More than a little upsetting was their "leader," a sometimes-hyper ex-Pharisee named Paul. These Christians were second-guessing their decision to believe in a dead guy who some said was resurrected from the dead. Like their ancestors before them, they were quick to look back to the old way of doing things and gold-plate it. The reading for day 5 is lengthy because the content needs to be taken in context. This is the crux of the reasoning, the case for Christ.

Read past the familiar and investigate the sometimes overlooked passages of these books.

READ

Day One	1 Peter 1–3
Day Two	1 Peter 4–5
Day Three	2 Peter 1–3
Day Four	Hebrews 1–3

Day Five   Hebrews 4–9
Day Six   Hebrews 10–11
Day Seven   Hebrews 12–13

CONSIDER

The book of Hebrews is among the most common texts used for sermons and devotions. It's unusual that the wordsmith didn't take credit for this work. He must have known and believed John the Baptist's mantra, "He must increase, but I must decrease" (John 3:30 ESV). This author knew the Old Testament words and believed that the "old system had found fulfillment in the new."[22] He wrote to assure his recipients that Christ was "better and superior" to the old ways, using the words fifteen times.[23] This author, like Mark, reminds us that when Jesus finished his task on Earth, he sat down at the right hand of God (Hebrews 1:3). The author establishes immediately who Jesus is.

These readings contain some of the most familiar, reassuring verses in the Bible. It asks a most probing question early in the letter: "What makes us think we can escape if we ignore this great salvation"? (Hebrews 2:3 NLT). In chapter 3, readers are reminded of the unbelief of their ancestors and the outcome. Reading this book with open heart and mind—is there any doubt that Christ offers a full and satisfying life?

Furthermore, Hebrews 2:18 reminds us that Jesus himself suffered and was tested. Because of His experience, He is more than capable of helping us. Peter's message was similar. Suffering is inevitable; it's our responsibility to deal with it like Jesus did. He uses the word *suffering* eleven times but reminds us sixteen times that suffering will bring Him glory. His second letter could be a handbook for the last days.

All three books discuss holiness and godliness. In 1 Peter 1:13–16 Peter echoes Moses' words from Leviticus 19:2: we must be holy because God is holy. Holiness means to be set apart. There has never been a greater command and never harder to achieve.

RESPOND

Define "this great salvation."

Compare your definition of suffering with that of the New Testament apostles.

What does holiness look like in your life?

Love Stories

LEARN

As we near the end of the year and the end of our Bible reading, we read two of the human love stories God chose to place in His Holy Word: Esther and Song of Songs. They both have a fairy tale content, but make no mistake, they are as inspired as any other portion of the Word.

You may remember in previous history readings that Esther's story takes place between chapters 6 and 7 of the book of Ezra. Esther, with her uncle and guardian, Mordecai, are members of the Jewish families taken into captivity. Through a series of misfortunes, they end up in Persia. In a strange turn of events, Esther becomes queen of Persia. Even stranger, God, who is never mentioned in the book, uses Esther to save the entire nation of Jews.

Solomon's Song of Songs is a book of love poetry between a young wife and her lover, Solomon. Which of the three hundred wives, we may wonder? It is believed that Solomon wrote it early in his life as king and probably was written to the Shulamite wife of his youth. The book describes a holy marriage. Apart from the world's view of this institution, God always had a plan for love between a man and a woman. Nick Page, in his book *The Map*, says there is much in the Old Testament about lust, perversion, shame, and rape. This is a book that celebrates what is good about love.[24]

READ

Day One	Song of Songs 1-3
Day Two	Song of Songs 4-6
Day Three	Song of Songs 7-8
Day Four	Esther 1-2
Day Five	Esther 3-5
Day Six	Esther 6-7
Day Seven	Esther 8-10

CONSIDER

The book of Esther is popular content for movies, stories, sermons, and devotions. The familiar story deserves a deeper look between the lines. The name of God is not mentioned once in the book of Esther, but His plan is woven between every line. The book is full of coincidence. Coincidence is defined as "a striking occurrence of two or more events at one time apparently by mere chance." Was Esther's life a series of coincidences?

Esther just happens to get rounded up with many others and taken to the palace after Queen Vashti just happened to make the king so mad, he threw her out. With all the girls to choose from, King Xerxes just happens to choose her to be queen. Her uncle just happens to overhear two guys plot to kill the king. The king just happens to have a sleepless night, rolls over, and just happens to pick up a scroll that reminds him of the time Mordecai saved his life. This king just happens to love Esther enough to get jealous when he sees Haman on top of her. That's a whole lot of events that just happened to happen. God knew what Haman would try to do, and before it happened, He set salvation in motion—in the very same way that He set salvation in motion as he watched Adam and Eve leave the garden.

The name Esther means "I will hide." In Deuteronomy 31:17 (NIV), God predicted that Israel would rebel, and He told Moses, " I will hide my face from them." Hidden never means not present. In Persia, captive Israel was never out of sight of God. Once again, He showed mercy and compassion on a people who were not deserving. Behind the scenes, He was orchestrating His plan for their good. Perhaps that is what is happening on your behalf right now.

RESPOND

What "coincidences" have happened in your life that you can now credit to God's providence?

What if Esther had given in to fear and not approached the king on behalf of her people?

What is your reaction to the Song of Songs? Why do you suppose it was included in the Holy Scriptures?

WEEK 52

The End of the Beginning

LEARN

At the conclusion of this week, we will have read the entire Bible. We can expect to feel accomplishment, relief, and pride, but there is also a bittersweet taste. The Word of God has become alive in our hearts and spirits. We have seen things we have missed in previous readings. Our hunger will not be satisfied; we will want more. The beloved disciple John understood those feelings.

As an old man living in Ephesus, he wrote three brief letters. He was responsible for starting several churches in the area, but the three letters written by John do not address a specific congregation. It is likely the churches he started were the recipients. His letters were straight talk about love and life. John wove the truths of the gospel into everyday existence. He encouraged others to do the same.

False teachings were a consistent problem for the early church, and every apostle in every letter addressed it. John was no different. Letter number one, 1 John, calls out these false teachers and insists that the children of God enjoy fellowship with their Father. Letter number two, 2 John, denounces false teachers again and warns the audience to walk in truth. This letter includes instruction about hospitality and support for traveling ministers. Gaius, identified as a "dear friend," received the third letter (3 John 1:1 NLT OR NIV). John describes Gaius as one who walks in the truth, is faithful, loving, and generous.

About five years later, John was imprisoned on the Isle of Patmos, a small island in the Aegean Sea about fifty miles southwest of Ephesus. By his own account he was exiled for preaching the Word of God and sharing his testimony regarding Jesus (Revelation 1:9). Among the most illiterate of people, a cursory awareness of the book of Revelation exists. Even among the most literate, most of the writing escapes understanding. Revelation requires much study and research, and much is available (see the Resources section at the end of this book). Nevertheless, to end this year, choose a user-friendly translation, ask the Holy Spirit to enhance your understanding, and read on.

READ

Day One   1 John 1-5
Day Two   2 and 3 John

CONSIDER

The book of Revelation has revealed those things that many believe are quickly approaching. Many find it uncomfortable, confusing, or downright frightening. The antidote is good teaching. Understanding and the truth revealed by the Holy Spirit will ease fear and give hope.

It is fitting that John was the author of this book. His previous letters pave the way to hear the hard message of Revelation. The first verse of his first letter is reassuring: "We proclaim to you the one who existed from the beginning, whom we have heard and seen. We saw him with our own eyes and touched him with our own hands. He is the Word of life" (1 John 1:1 NLT). The rest of this letter is written in love and with a message of correction, much like a parent would discipline a child for their own good. John doesn't want anyone to sin or love the world. He is steadfast that nothing, nothing compares to life in Christ. "See how very much our Father loves us, for he calls us his children" (1 John 3:1 NLT). He reminds us that we have complete confidence in approaching Jesus. He uses the word *truth* repeatedly in all three letters. Let there be no doubt that "truth" is the gospel of Jesus Christ.

John may have read Paul's letter to the Ephesians long before his own words truly spoke the truth in love. John was the ultimate example of speaking hard truths wrapped in love.

Today it is our responsibility to speak the truth. Not my truth or your truth, those do not exist. The world says truth is a fact or belief accepted as truth, but Jesus says, " I am . . . the truth" (John 14:6 niv).

John 20:29 (nlt) says, " Blessed are those who believe without seeing me." We are blessed when we believe. It is our directive to proclaim the truth of Jesus through the words in His Word. We know Him because He is the Word made flesh, and we have dwelt in that Word for 365 days.

RESPOND

How do you describe truth? How can you declare it in love?

How has reading the entire Bible changed your perception of it?

What part of Scripture were you surprised that you enjoyed?

YOU DID IT!

ADDITIONAL RESOURCES

Baxter, J. Sidlow. *Baxter's Explore the Book*. Grand Rapids: Zondervan, 2010.

Bible Hub. https://www.biblehub.com.

Dictionary.com https://www.dictionary.com/

Daymond R. *Revelation: God's Word for the Biblically Inept*.

Lancaster, PA: Starburst Publishers, 1997.

Eyewitness.Bible Series accessed April 5, 2021 https://www.rightnowmedia.org/Search?q=Eyewitness%20Bible%20Series

Fee, Gordon D., and Mark L. Strauss. *How to Choose a Translation for All Its Worth: A Guide to Understanding and Using Bible Versions*. Grand Rapids: Zondervan, 2009.

Henry, Matthew. *Matthew Henry's Concise Commentary on the Whole Bible*. Nashville: Thomas Nelson, 2003.

Lotz, Anne G. T*he Daniel Prayer: Prayer That Moves Heaven and Changes Nations*. Grand Rapids: Zondervan, 2016.

Lyons, Rebekah. *You Are Free: Be Who You Already Are*. Grand Rapids: Zondervan, 2017.

Maclaren, Alexander. "Maclaren's Expositions." https://
biblescan.com/search.php?q=MacLaren%27s+Expositions.
Accessed April 8, 2021.

McDowell, Landon. Accessed April 5, 2021, https://www.
rightnowmedia.org/Search?q=Landon%20MacDonald.

Nicholson, Jabe. "Scripture Snapshots." Accessed
April 5, 2021. https://www.rightnowmedia.org/
Search?q=Scripture%20Snapshotsge, Nick. *The MAP:
Making the Bible Meaningful, Accessible, Practical.* Grand
Rapids: Zondervan, 2004.

Stamps, Donald C., and J. W. Adams. *The Full Life Study
Bible: New International Version.* Grand Rapids: Zondervan,
1992.

Visit

https://www.tonyaann.com

for additional resources and resource reviews.

Receive a downloadable Bible Reading chart FREE.

ENDNOTES

1   Donald C. Stamps and J. W. Adams, *The Full Life Study Bible: New International Version* (Grand Rapids, MI: Zondervan, 1992), 1412.

2   H. D. M. Spence and Joseph S. Exell, eds., *Pulpit Commentary,* accessed July 5,2021, https://biblehub.com/commentaries/pulpit/joshua/5.htm.

3   "George Santayana Quotes," BrainyQuote.com, https://www.brainyquote.com/quotes/george_santayana_101521.

4   Donald C. Stamps and J. W. Adams, *The Full Life Study Bible,* 973.

5   Jabe Nicholson, "Scripture Snapshots," section six, RightNowMedia.org, accessed July 5, 2021, https://www.rightnowmedia.org/Content/Series/448609.

6   Donald C. Stamps and J. W. Adams, *The Full Life Study Bible*, 1079.

7   Donald C. Stamps and J. W. Adams, *The Full Life Study Bible*, 1748.

8   Alexander MacLaren, "MacLaren's Expositions," BibleHub.com, accessed July 5, 2021, https://biblehub.com/commentaries/mark/16-19.htm.

9   J. Sidlow Baxter, *Baxter's Explore the Book* (Grand Rapids, MI: Zondervan, 1960; 2010).

10   Matthew Henry, "Matthew Henry's Commentary," BibleHub.com, accessed July 5, 2021, https://biblehub.com/commentaries/mhc/job/32.htm.

11   Rebekah Lyons, *You Are Free: Be Who You Already Are* (Grand Rapids, MI: Zondervan, 2017), 22.

12   Nick Page, *The MAP: Making the Bible Meaningful, Accessible, Practical* (Grand Rapids, MI: Zondervan, 2004), 196.

13   Landon MacDonald, "Major Prophets," RightNowMedia. com, accessed July 5, 2021, https://www.rightnowmedia. org/Content/Series/468305.

14   Jabe Nicholson, "Scripture Snapshots," section four, accessed July 5, 2021, https://www.rightnowmedia.org/Content/ Series/347569.

15   H. D. M. Spence and Joseph S. Exell, eds., *Pulpit Commentary*, accessed July 5, 2021, https://biblehub.com/ commentaries/pulpit/2_thessalonians/1.htm.

16   Nick Page, *The MAP*, 233.

17   Nick Page, *The MAPl*, 369.

18   Charles Ellicott, *Ellicott's Commentary on the Whole Bible*, BibleHub.com, accessed July 5, 2021, https://biblehub.com/ commentaries/ellicott/acts/4.htm.

19   Jabe Nicholson, "The Poetry Books – Scripture Snapshots," session 3, accessed July 5, 2021, https://www. rightnowmedia.org/Content/Series/347559?episode=3.

20   Evan Howard, "Praying Scripture," BibleGateway.com, accessed July 5, 2021, https://www.biblegateway.com/ resources/scripture-engagement/praying-scripture/home.

21   Landon MacDonald, "Books of Wisdom," session 4, accessed July 5, 2021, https://www.rightnowmedia.org/ Content/Series/468315?episode=4.

22   Nick Page, *The MAP*, 364.

23   Nick Page, *The MAP*, 364.

24   Nick Page, *The MAP*, 173.